Acclaim for Nora Ephron's

IMAGINARY FRIENDS

"Nora Ephron has written a very clever play. A sophisticated evening of cheeky merriment." —*New York* magazine

"An irreverent, stylish joyride, wickedly entertaining."
—*Time Out*

"Scripted with razor-sharp wit. . . . Takes cattiness soaring to transcendent heights." —*USA Today*

"A highly engaging vaudeville, part dual biography, part witty appreciation, part extended argument, part send-up and part rueful meditation on vanity, morality, the stories we tell and the lives we manufacture. Inspired. A form-breaker."
—*Chicago Sun-Times*

"A sly and deftly poised entertainment. . . . Artfully theatrical."
—*San Francisco Chronicle*

NORA EPHRON

IMAGINARY FRIENDS

Nora Ephron is the author of *Crazy Salad*, *Heartburn*, *Wallflower at the Orgy*, and *Scribble Scribble*. She has received Academy Award nominations for Best Original Screenplay for *When Harry Met Sally*, *Silkwood*, and *Sleepless in Seattle*, which she also directed. She lives in New York City with her husband, writer Nicholas Pileggi.

Also *by* Nora Ephron

FICTION
Heartburn

ESSAYS
Wallflower at the Orgy
Crazy Salad
Scribble Scribble
Nora Ephron Collected

SCREENPLAYS
Silkwood (with Alice Arlen)
Heartburn
Cookie (with Alice Arlen)
When Harry Met Sally
My Blue Heaven
This Is My Life (with Delia Ephron)
Sleepless in Seattle (with David S. Ward and Jeff Arch)
Mixed Nuts (with Delia Ephron)
Michael (with Jim Quinlan, Pete Dexter, and Delia Ephron)
You've Got Mail (with Delia Ephron)
Hanging Up (with Delia Ephron)

IMAGINARY FRIENDS

IMAGINARY
FRIENDS

NORA EPHRON

Lyrics by Craig Carnelia

VINTAGE BOOKS
A Division of Random House, Inc.
New York

A VINTAGE ORIGINAL, APRIL 2003

All inquiries concerning performance rights in the work appearing herein should
be addressed to the author's agent, International Creative Management, Inc.,
Attn: Sam Cohn, 40 West 57th Street, New York, NY 10019.

Lyrics by Craig Carnelia

Library of Congress Cataloging-in-Publication Data
Ephron, Nora.
Imaginary friends / Nora Ephron.
p. cm.
"A Vintage original"—T.p. verso.
ISBN: 1-4000-3422-1
1. Hellman, Lillian, 1906-—Drama. 2. McCarthy, Mary, 1912-—
Drama. 3. Libel and slander—Drama. 4. Literary quarrels—Drama.
5. Women authors—Drama. I. Title.

PS3555.P5I45 2003
812'.54—dc21
2002041171

Book design by Oksana Kushnir

www.vintagebooks.com

Printed in the United States of America
10 9 8 7 6 5 4 3

for Nick

INTRODUCTION

On a January night in 1980, Lillian Hellman was in bed, watching *The Dick Cavett Show,* when Mary McCarthy hurled her famously vicious remark about Hellman into the ether. "Are there any writers you think are overrated?" Cavett asked. McCarthy replied: "The only one I can think of is a holdover like Lillian Hellman, who I think is tremendously overrated, a bad writer, and dishonest writer, but she really belongs to the past. . . ." "What is so dishonest about her?" Cavett asked. "Everything," McCarthy said. "But I said once in some interview that every word she writes is a lie, including 'and' and 'the.'"

That remark, and what followed—a $2.25 million lawsuit Hellman filed against McCarthy—brought to a head almost forty-five years of skirmishing between the two women. Some of it is easy to document because it was in print. Mary, writing in *Partisan Review* in 1946, attacked Lillian's work. Lillian responded in a *Paris Review* interview in 1964. Mary struck again in a *People* magazine interview in 1979. And so forth. But where and exactly how the enmity began is maddeningly elusive. Did the two women meet for the first time at a dinner party in 1936? Perhaps. Did they argue at that dinner about the Spanish civil war and the incredibly brave civil war martyr Andres Nin? Mary McCarthy argued with someone at a dinner party about the Spanish civil war and Andres Nin, because she wrote a short story about a dinner party where a young woman remarkably like Mary McCarthy has an argument with someone about the

Spanish civil war and Andres Nin. Was that someone Lillian Hellman? Or did McCarthy confuse Hellman with another Stalinist, named Leane Zugsmith?

Did their enmity begin not because of politics but for more personal reasons? Perhaps. For it seems that one night in 1936, while Mary McCarthy was living with *Partisan Review* editor Philip Rahv, Lillian Hellman met Rahv and attempted to seduce him. When he returned to the apartment he was sharing with McCarthy, he claimed he hadn't actually slept with Hellman because he didn't find her attractive. The incident, McCarthy told one of her biographers, was the only real fight of her relationship with Rahv. Was Rahv telling the truth? McCarthy believed him. Whether she was right to (do you?) is another mystery.

The two women clearly and absolutely met at Sarah Lawrence College in 1948, and they most definitely had a fight there. Was the fight about the incredibly brave Andres Nin, as McCarthy claimed? Did McCarthy spend her life picking fights about the incredibly brave Andres Nin? Did she confuse the fight she'd had at the dinner party years earlier with the fight they had at Sarah Lawrence? There's no way to know. Years later, when Mary's biographers went to poet Stephen Spender—who was supposedly there—for the details, he turned out to be entirely confused about the episode. He thought it had taken place at his home. It had actually taken place at the home of Harold Taylor, then president of Sarah Lawrence—and Spender hadn't been there at all. It seems, in fact, that there were not one but two fights that day: one at Taylor's, and one later, at Spender's. Or were there?

I began thinking about writing something about Lillian Hellman and Mary McCarthy a few years ago, when I read two biographies of McCarthy, *Writing Dangerously* by Carol Brightman, and *Seeing Mary Plain* by Frances Kiernan. I'd never met McCarthy, but I'd known Lillian Hellman. I met her when I was a journalist, and I have to say that for several years I was under her spell. Lillian was fun, a wonderful hostess, cook, correspondent, and storyteller. It was quite a while before I began to suspect that the fabulous stories she entertained her friends with were, to be polite about it, stories. When she sued McCarthy years afterward, I wasn't surprised. She was sick by then, and legally blind. And her anger—the anger that was her favorite accessory—had turned wearisome, even to those who were loyal to her.

When I read the biographies of McCarthy, it crossed my mind that there might be something to write about McCarthy and Hellman and their collision. At first I thought of some sort of high-minded television series—six or seven parts, say—that told the story of their parallel, albeit dissimilar, lives. Mary, of course, was an orphan, Catholic, abused. Lillian was an only child, Jewish, spoiled. Mary was beautiful. Lillian was not. Mary became an intellectual and a star in a world that had a pathological distrust not just of commercial success but also of stars. Lillian was the epitome of the commercial playwright, rich and famous. Mary was a Trotskyite, Lillian a Stalinist. (Lillian was what's known as an unreconstructed Stalinist. As she lay dying, someone I know said to her, "Well, Lillian, what do you think of Joe Stalin now?" She replied, "You can't make an omelette without breaking eggs.") Perhaps most crucial, Mary was a critic, a great critic. Lillian was not a great playwright, but she was a great dramatist. It seemed so extraordinary that these two women—who'd written so much, who'd led such rich and complicated lives, who'd almost never been in the same room, who truly couldn't stand each other—had ended up, in some terrible way, linked forever.

But every time I thought about this television series—now called something fabulously pretentious (in my imagination), like "Two American Women"—I became tired. The words "Who can I get to write it?" kept crossing my mind. The last thing I wanted to work on was a long project that would end up seeming like docudrama. And I'd seen quite a lot of dramatizations of Lillian's life, onstage and in film. She'd been played by Jane Fonda, Elaine Stritch, Linda Lavin, Zoe Caldwell, and Judy Davis. But none of it had really caught Lillian, the Lillian I knew, anyway; and all of it seemed so constricted, even by the loose rules of biography.

And what was to be done about "the facts"—the poor, distressed facts of these women's lives? In her autobiographical writing, McCarthy was painfully honest. But what, for example, had actually gone on during McCarthy's terrible marriage to Edmund Wilson? McCarthy spent her life coming up with a succession of excuses for why she married him in the first place, none of them remotely satisfying, apparently even to her. The divorce depositions of McCarthy and Wilson completely contradict each other. Lillian, on the other hand, had no interest whatsoever in the truth; her attitude toward it is probably best summed up by one of her characters in *The Little Foxes*, who says: "God forgives those who invent what they need." The story of Julia in *Pentimento*, which became the basis of a critically acclaimed movie, was certainly a total invention. And the Julia effect spilled over into a great deal of Lillian's autobiography—every bit of it became suspect. As Gore Vidal famously said of Hellman and Dashiell Hammett: "Did anyone ever see them together?"

And then one day I was talking to someone about Hellman and McCarthy, and he said, "Could it be a play?" A play? I'd never written a play. I'd always wanted to write one; I'd been an avid theatergoer all my life. I'd always hoped that something would cross my brain that was a play, but what was a play? If a play was six people trapped for arbitrary reasons in a summer house with a lot of French doors, I was out of luck. Years ago I'd attended a program at the Actors Studio that was meant to encourage playwriting. It was interesting, actually: every week someone would turn up with a play he'd written, actors would perform it, usually at a table read, and then the people in the audience—most of them writers—would attack it. The writer Harold Brodkey was part of the group, and no matter what the play's subject was, he usually accused the playwright of being anti-Semitic. This process did not seem to me to encourage playwriting, although for a while I thought about writing a play that took place at a table read at the Actors Studio and that included a character not unlike Harold Brodkey. In any case, after a while I stopped going to the Actors Studio and resigned myself to the possibility that my relationship with the theater would always and forever be as a member of the audience.

But Lillian and Mary, a play? A cartoon lightbulb lit up in my head. Of course: a play. I knew where it took place, and I even knew the first line. I could imagine McCarthy and Hellman—not necessarily as friends but at least in conversation. I could write an entire scene about what happened at Sarah Lawrence, and turn it into a scene about how impossible it was to know what happened at Sarah Lawrence. I could write about a subject that has interested me since my days as a magazine journalist: women and what they do to each other. I could write about McCarthy's love of the truth—which she turned into a religion—and about Hellman's way with a story, which she turned into a pathology. I could do it, I hoped, without taking sides. (How could you take sides, after all? They were both wrong. And, at the same time, they were both right.) And I could perhaps end up with something that was not the truth, and not the story, but something else. To begin with, a play.

IMAGINARY FRIENDS

Imaginary Friends was first produced at the Old Globe Theatre in San Diego, where it opened on September 29, 2002. The production then moved to the Ethel Barrymore Theatre, New York, where it was presented by USA Ostar Theatricals and opened on December 12, 2002, with the following cast:

LILLIAN HELLMAN	Swoosie Kurtz
MARY MCCARTHY	Cherry Jones
THE MAN	Harry Groener
A WOMAN	Anne Pitoniak
ABBY KAISER & others	Anne Allgood
LEO & others	Bernard Dotson
MRS. STILLMAN & others	Rosena M. Hill
BEGUINE DANCER & others	Gina Lamparelli
FACT & others	Dirk Lumbard
FICTION & others	Peter Marx
VIC & others	Perry Ojeda
FIZZY & others	Karyn Quackenbush

Directed by	Jack O'Brien
Choreographed by	Jerry Mitchell
Music by	Marvin Hamlisch
Lyrics by	Craig Carnelia
Designed by	Michael Levine
Lighting by	Kenneth Posner

CHARACTERS

Lillian Hellman
Mary McCarthy
Max Hellman
Fizzy
Uncle Myers
Dashiell Hammett
Edmund Wilson
Philip Rahv
James T. Farrell
Harold Taylor
Stephen Spender
Sarah Lawrence student
Black maid
Fact
Fiction
Dick Cavett
Paris Reporter
Abby Kaiser
Norman Mailer
Mary's lawyer
Muriel Gardiner (A Woman)

In the original production, one actor played the parts of Max Hellman, Uncle Myers, Dashiell Hammett, Edmund Wilson, Philip Rahv, James T. Farrell, the black maid, Norman Mailer, and Mary's lawyer.

ACT I

Scene 1

A bare stage.

We see two women smoking. They are LILLIAN HELLMAN *and* MARY MCCARTHY. *They're wearing suits and heels.*

LILLIAN: Did we ever meet?

MARY: Once or twice.

LILLIAN: I don't really remember.

MARY: Well, then I don't remember, either.

LILLIAN: All right. Where was it?

MARY: At Sarah Lawrence College. Stephen Spender invited us to speak—

LILLIAN: *I* was invited. You turned up.

MARY: You thought I was a student because I looked quite young.

LILLIAN: I didn't even notice you.

MARY: My point. I walked onto the sunporch, and you were telling all of them a huge lie—

LILLIAN: Naturally—

MARY: —about the Spanish civil war. I couldn't bear it. You were brainwashing them, and they were looking at you like wide-eyed converts. So I interrupted and corrected you. And we had a fight. *[To the audience.]* And I remember that on her bare arms, she had a great many bracelets, gold and silver—

A long string with a hook on the end falls from the rafters with a bunch of gold and silver bracelets dangling from it. LILLIAN *puts them on.*

—and they began to tremble in her fury and surprise at being caught red-handed in a lie.

LILLIAN *holds out her arm and makes the bracelets jangle against one another, louder and louder.*

LILLIAN: Like that?

MARY: Exactly. The incident at Sarah Lawrence was in 1948. I was teaching there at the time—

LILLIAN: I never had to do that. I *did* teach, but I never *had* to teach. Although once, after I testified, after I stood up on the bad morning before the House Un-American Activities Committee and said—

LILLIAN AND MARY: *[Together.]* "I cannot and will not cut my conscience to fit this year's fashions." *[A beat as* LILLIAN *looks at* MARY.*]*

LILLIAN: You're not suggesting I never said it.

MARY: Of course you said it.

LILLIAN: Fine. After I said it, and had to sell the farm—

MARY: It wasn't a farm. It was a house—

LILLIAN: It was too a farm. It was upstate—

MARY: Westchester County is not upstate—

LILLIAN: There were cows and chickens—

MARY: Fine. It was a farm—

LILLIAN: —after that I had no money—

MARY: —and no place to live but your New York town house—

LILLIAN: *[Plunging on.]*—I had no money to speak of, but I didn't teach. I went to work part-time at Macy's, selling groceries.

> MARY *looks at her, entirely unbelieving. After a beat, she turns back to the audience and plunges on.*

MARY: Stephen Spender invited us to speak at Sarah Lawrence because we were—

LILLIAN: Women. Let's face it.

MARY: You are so right. They were having a writers' conference, and they couldn't invite only men—it was a women's college, after all—

LILLIAN: We were the logical choices.

MARY: There were others.

LILLIAN: Who?

MARY: There were plenty of others.

LILLIAN: Hmmph.

MARY: Martha Gellhorn.

LILLIAN: She was good.

MARY: She was first-rate.

LILLIAN: During the war. But then what? She took herself out of the running. She stayed in England, doomed to be known forever as Ernest Hemingway's third wife. And no one reads her any more. Jean Stafford.

MARY: Yes, I suppose Jean Stafford.

LILLIAN: Well, I don't suppose Jean Stafford. I brought her up only to make myself seem open-minded.

MARY: And she drank herself right out of the competition, didn't she?

LILLIAN: Yes she did.

MARY: And no one reads *her* anymore, either.

LILLIAN: No one reads any of us.

MARY: "We all lead our lives more or less in vain. . . ." I said that only a few months before I died. I was trying to be brave . . . about cancer, and death, and the sense that it had all been . . . for nothing. To have no one know who you are after all that typing—

LILLIAN: —all that typing and thinking and drinking and flirting and fucking and feuding. But some of it was fun, wasn't it? We didn't do all that typing and thinking and drinking and flirting and fucking and feuding just so people would know who we were, did we?

A pause while they think about it.

When would you say that you and I started feuding?

MARY: From the beginning. And then, of course, the lawsuit. Lillian Hellman versus Mary McCarthy.

LILLIAN: We never liked each other.

MARY: Yes, I was always hearing you didn't like me.

LILLIAN: Well, I was always hearing you'd written mean things about me.

MARY: I didn't write much about you.

LILLIAN: When you did, it was always mean. But we rarely saw one another. That night when I turned on the television set, I had no idea what you were going to look like after all those years. I was watching, you know. I saw you say it. I was lying in bed, completely happy at seeing how badly you'd aged, and then you said it.

And now, on the scrim behind them, we see a television show projected: MARY *being interviewed by* DICK CAVETT.

> DICK CAVETT: Are there any writers you think are overrated?
>
> MARY: The only one I can think of is a holdover like Lillian Hellman, who I think is tremendously overrated, a bad writer, and dishonest writer, but she really belongs to the past. . . .
>
> DICK CAVETT: What is dishonest about her?
>
> MARY: Everything. But I said once in some interview that every word she writes is a lie, including "and" and "the."

A beat.

MARY: Most people outgrow the feuding, don't you think?

LILLIAN: Well, I never outgrew it.

MARY: Nor I.

LILLIAN: My anger—

MARY: My honesty—

LILLIAN: "You must choose your enemies well."

MARY: Who said that?

LILLIAN: Goethe. It's my favorite line from Goethe. I once read a book about two U-boats. It was written with alternating chapters, and the first was about the German U-boat. The captain woke up in the morning and trimmed his mustache and spoke to the cook about sausages. Then came the chapter about the English U-boat, and the captain woke up in the morning and looked at the starboard diesel and spoke to the cook about kippers. This went on throughout the day, day after day, alternating, until the boats finally met up with one another.

MARY: And then what happened? Did they collide?

LILLIAN: They did collide. Shall I begin?

MARY: Why not? You came first.

LILLIAN *looks around. We hear music.*

Music?

LILLIAN: Why not? We have musicians. *[Beat.]* I need . . . a fig tree.

She exits.

Scene 2

Childhood.

We see a big wooden house with a front porch. Next to it is a big fig tree.

The ENSEMBLE *does a cakewalk onto the stage as we hear a New Orleans band start to play. Maybe the band comes onto the stage, like a New Orleans parade procession.*

Projected on the back of the stage, we see the words "New Orleans" and a picture of baby Lillian.

And the ENSEMBLE *starts to sing "The Fig Tree Rag."*

ENSEMBLE:
    THERE'S SOMETHIN' HAPPENIN' IN DIXIE
    I'M FROM DIXIE SO I KNOW
    WE GOT A RAG WE CALL "THE FIG TREE"
    FOR THAT BIG TREE THAT WE GROW
    AND WHEN WE'RE HOPPIN' ON THE BAYOU
    I DEFY YOU TO BE STILL
    GET YOU A RAGGY TUNE
    GET YOU A CAJUN MOON
    GET YOU A JACK OR A JILL

    COME ON ALONG
    WE'RE GONNA DO THE FIG TREE RAG
    YOUR BODY GONNA ZIG AND ZAG
    TAKE A LOOK AT
    EV'RY CHAP AND EV'RY CHIPPY

ALL ALONG THE MISSISSIPPI
DOIN' THE DANCE
THEY'RE DANCIN' TO THE FIG TREE RAG
I WANNA DO THE FIG TREE RAG WITH YOU.

LILLIAN *enters. She's playing herself as a child and wearing a white dress almost identical to the one in the picture. The effect should be half baby, half Baby Snooks. She walks toward the tree.*

LILLIAN: I was the sweetest-smelling baby in New Orleans. You probably heard that about me, and it is one hundred percent true. My father was a traveling salesman, so my mother and I lived in the Garden District with my two aunts, Jenny and Hannah, who owned a boardinghouse. I had a Negro nurse named Sophronia, who took care of me until I was six, when we began to spend half the year in New York and the other half back in New Orleans. Behind my aunts' boardinghouse was a fig tree, an enormous fig tree. It was quite a ways from the house, and it was so leafy you couldn't be seen. So I rigged up a seat for myself, and a set of pulleys for soda pop and books, and I would sit up there and read and spy on the orphans down the block, who seemed wildly glamorous—

ENSEMBLE:
COME WITH ME
UP IN THE TREE
UP IN THE TREE
ALL OUR TROUBLES ARE FAR AWAY
SWING AND SWAY
UP IN THE TREE
UP IN THE TREE WE'LL STAY

LILLIAN: There was Frances, whose father had been killed by the
   Mafia, and Louis, who took me to Mass, and Pancho, who
   once gave me a lock of his hair and then pushed me into the
   gutter, which was without question the most romantic thing
   that had ever happened—so romantic that I put the lock
   of hair into the back of a wristwatch my father had just
   given me for my birthday. And my watch stopped.

   LILLIAN *climbs into a seat at the base of the tree and raises
   herself into it.*

ENSEMBLE:
   SO IF YOU'RE LOOKING FOR A HAVEN
   WITH A CRAVIN' TO FULFILL
   I'LL SHOW YOU WHAT HEAVEN MEANS
   MEET ME IN NEW ORLEANS
   I'LL KEEP ON HUMMIN' UNTIL
   YA GET HERE

   COME ON ALONG
   WE'RE GONNA DO THE FIG TREE RAG
   YOUR BODY GONNA ZIG AND ZAG
   YA GOT ME THINKIN'
   THIS IS WHERE IT ALL WAS LEADIN'
   IN THE GARDEN KNOWN AS EDEN
   ADAM AND EVE
   WERE TRYIN' OUT THE FIG TREE RAG
   I WANNA DO THE FIG TREE RAG WITH YOU
   WITH YOU

   WE'RE CRANKIN' LIKE A HURDY GURDY

LILLIAN:
   FLAPPIN' LIKE A PERDY BIRDY

ENSEMBLE:

DOIN' THE FIG TREE RAG

LILLIAN: From the tree I could also watch the people who lived in the boardinghouse—Mrs. Stillman, who was crazy, and Carrie, the cook, who plucked chickens in the yard, and Sarah and Fizzy, two dizzy sisters who were always picking on me and giggling over nothing. "She's so wiiiiild and willful," they'd say, and just stand there together and giggle.

FIZZY *comes out of the boardinghouse and sits down on the porch.*

That's Fizzy. Giggle for everyone, Fizzy.

FIZZY *giggles.* FIZZY *takes out a fan and fans herself in a kind of exaggerated southern way.* MAX HELLMAN, *Lillian's father, comes from around the back of the house and looks at* FIZZY *as she sits there.*

And that's my father.

LILLIAN *hides behind some leaves, and we don't see her in the tree.* FIZZY *turns and sees* MAX HELLMAN.

FIZZY: Max! What a surprise. When did you get back?

MAX HELLMAN: Train just got in. Beautiful morning, isn't it? Even prettier now that I see you.

FIZZY: *[Giggles again.]* Oh, Max!

The leaves in the tree rustle wildly, but FIZZY *and* MAX HELLMAN *don't seem to notice.*

MAX HELLMAN: What were you thinking about?

FIZZY: Just now? Summertime, and my mama's hummingbird
garden. Sarah and I used to sit still as statues on the stone
bench and see if we could get the birds to buzz around our
heads. Once I put a piece of honeysuckle in my mouth—

MAX HELLMAN *suddenly kisses* FIZZY, *a long, passionate
kiss.* LILLIAN *spreads the branches of the tree just a little and
peeks out wide-eyed at what's happening. Then she closes
them over herself again.*

MAX HELLMAN: I missed you so much. *[Beat.]* Can I see you this
afternoon?

FIZZY: Two o'clock.

MAX HELLMAN: Corner of Jackson Street.

FIZZY *rushes into the house and closes the door.* MAX HELL-
MAN *walks off. A long beat.* LILLIAN *falls from the fig tree.
Splat. A horrible noise. She lies face down on the ground.
And now we see the real* LILLIAN *walk onstage and pick up
the* LILLIAN *that fell from the tree—which turns out to be a
large stuffed doll of* LILLIAN. *She carries it to the front
porch, where she sits. She puts her hand melodramatically
over her nose.*

LILLIAN: I broke my nose. So I went running off to find my old
nurse, Sophronia. I told her I'd seen Fizzy and my father
kissing each other, and I decided to kill myself. Sophronia
bandaged me up and told me that I must never ever tell anyone about Fizzy. I promised her I never would. A few min-
utes later, as she walked me home, she said, "Don't go

through life making trouble for people." I said, "If I tell you I won't tell anyone about Fizzy, I won't." *[*LILLIAN *stands up, carrying the doll. Then she walks into the house and closes the door.]*

The words "New Orleans" vanish from the scrim and are replaced with "Seattle," and some sort of music begins. The baby picture of LILLIAN *changes to one of* MARY MCCARTHY. MARY *comes onstage carrying a large doll of herself dressed like the little girl in the picture. She walks over to the musicians and looks at them.*

MARY: *[To the musicians.]* Please don't. *[They stop playing.]* My father was a lawyer, although he never really practiced law. He was sick and home most of the time, and he read me stories in the daytime, and once, when we were together, we heard a nightingale sing, I remember that. My mother was beautiful, and she had three more children, my brothers, and one day when I was six years old, we all got on the train to go to Minneapolis to visit my father's parents, who were rich. It was during the influenza pandemic, and we all caught it on the train, and my parents died.

The word on the scrim changes to "Minneapolis."

No one told us they'd died. We got off the train in Minneapolis, and there were nurses and ambulances waiting, and I woke up weeks later and everything was different. We were orphans. Not that we'd ever heard the word, and not that anyone had to tell us, really, because they told us in every way—there was to be no jam for the toast, and why anyone had ever let us have it in the first place no one knew, and "Sit up straight" and "Right this minute" and "Children should be seen but not heard," especially spoiled children—that was the problem, you see, we were spoiled, like food that had been left out too long. Something would have to be done with us, but what? And then, finally, a solution—a great-aunt had just married, to everyone's enormous relief, for she was old and plain as a wet sidewalk, and she and her new husband, Myers, were given a small house to live in, and the four of us wretched children. And still no one told us our parents were dead. No one ever told us. For a while they said Mommy and Daddy had gone to get well in the hospital. And then they stopped saying things like that, and it was assumed we all knew, even though we'd never been told.

UNCLE MYERS *walks out of the house.*

That's Uncle Myers.

UNCLE MYERS *takes out a leather razor strop and flicks it against the porch railing with a sharp snap.*

And that's his razor strop.

UNCLE MYERS: Mary—

MARY: Yes, Uncle—

UNCLE MYERS: I gave your brother a tin butterfly several days ago.

MARY: I know. From a Cracker Jack box. Will you get me one? Please? I would love one so much.

UNCLE MYERS: He can't find it. Have you seen it anywhere?

MARY: No. So it's lost?

UNCLE MYERS: Well, that all depends, doesn't it . . . [UNCLE MYERS *flicks his strop against the railing again. Then he walks into the house.*]

MARY: The last thing I remember about my father was that I was sitting with him on the train.

We hear the sound of a train.

Everyone else is sick, tossing in their sleeping berths, but we're not, we're sitting there together, and I feel so proud of my father—the conductor tried to throw us off the train because so many of us are sick, but my father had a gun and wouldn't let him. Now we're riding through the Rockies, and he's saying that sometimes there are boulders that tumble down and crush the train and kill all the passengers. I remember it so clearly—the moment my father lifts me up so I'm standing on the seat, looking out the window as the mountains rush past. My heart is absolutely filled with fear that we'll all be squashed flat, but I feel completely safe because I'm in his arms—

The sound of the train dies away.

But it never happened. My father was sick long before we rode through the Rockies, and he couldn't possibly have told me anything about boulders. And no one tried to throw us off the train, and my father didn't have a gun, and there are no nightingales in North America.

UNCLE MYERS *comes out of the house again with the strop.*

UNCLE MYERS: Mary—

He hits the strop against the railing with a sharp snap.

BLACKOUT.

Scene 3

A nightclub.

Two bars onstage, each with a BARTENDER *mixing martinis. We're in a wonderful nightclub. The* BARTENDERS *are wearing white jackets that exactly match what the bartenders wear in an early scene from* The Thin Man.

On the scrim are the words "New York."

And now we see LILLIAN *and* MARY, *both in their late twenties and chic in simple black dresses, sitting on bar stools at their respective bars, as the* BARTENDERS *pour their perfect drinks into stemmed glasses.*

LILLIAN *and* MARY *each light a cigarette and blow smoke.*

The BARTENDERS *sing "A Smoke, A Drink, and You."*

BARTENDERS:
  A SMOKE, A DRINK, AND YOU
  A HAUNTING BEGUINE

AT THE START OF A SCENE FOR TWO
YOU OFFER A LIGHT RIGHT ON CUE
A SMOKE, A DRINK, AND YOU

WE JOKE, WE WINK, WE WOO
THE UNIVERSE SPINS
AS A CORKSCREW BEGINS TO SCREW
THE BARTENDERS FADE OUT OF VIEW
A SMOKE, A DRINK, AND YOU

COCKTAILS ARE FLOWING
AND SMOKE RINGS ARE BLOWING
AND SOMEHOW YOU KNOW WHAT TO DO
I'M HIGH AS THE MOON IS
AND EVEN THE TUNE IS ASCENDING
YOU STIR ME AND SHAKE ME
THE HEIGHTS THAT YOU TAKE ME
ARE SO VERY NEW
AND THEN YOU SHOW ME A VIEW
WITHOUT ENDING

Music continues. The BARTENDERS *pour another drink into* MARY's *and* LILLIAN's *glasses, and each lights another cigarette.*

MARY: Vassar.

LILLIAN: NYU.

MARY: Graduated.

LILLIAN: Dropped out.

MARY: Married.

LILLIAN: Married.

BARTENDERS:
THEY'LL BE ETERNALLY TRUE

MARY: Divorced.

LILLIAN: Divorced.

MARY: New York.

LILLIAN: New York.

MARY: I slept with Philip Rahv.

LILLIAN: I slept with Philip Rahv.

BARTENDERS:
THEY SLEPT WITH PHILIP RAHV

MARY: You did not sleep with Philip Rahv—

LILLIAN: Once. Once was enough.

BARTENDERS:
A SMOKE, A DRINK, AND YOU

LILLIAN *and* MARY *drain their drinks. The* BARTENDERS *pour each of them another.*

MARY: I was very beautiful.

LILLIAN: I was not.

MARY: And very smart.

LILLIAN: Whip-smart.

MARY: Cold eye.

LILLIAN: Sharp tongue.

MARY: Sharp tongue.

LILLIAN: Cold eye.

MARY: Loved danger.

LILLIAN: Loved trouble.

MARY: Loved fights.

LILLIAN: *Loved* fights.

MARY: Quick.

LILLIAN: Just as quick.

MARY: And very beautiful.

LILLIAN: I wish I'd been beautiful.

MARY: I wish I'd been rich.

LILLIAN: But if I'd been beautiful, would any of it have happened?

MARY: And if I'd been rich—

LILLIAN: You'd have been sued many more times than you were. Philip Rahv wanted to sue you and so did Edmund Wilson and so did all those girls you went to Vassar with. Even your own uncle wanted to sue you.

MARY: You wanted to sue me.

LILLIAN: And I did sue you. That's where all this is leading.

MARY: And I didn't have enough money to defend myself.

LILLIAN: But people gave it to you. People felt sorry for you and gave it to you. People who hated me gave it to you. People who hated you gave it to you because they hated me more. And you took the money—

MARY: For my lawyers.

LILLIAN: Hmmph.

A beat.

MARY: I was very beautiful.

LILLIAN: And I was not. But I had something.

A tall man walks up to the bar, and a BARTENDER *starts to mix him a drink. This is* DASHIELL HAMMETT.

DASHIELL HAMMETT:
A MAN APPEARS ON CUE

BARTENDERS:
    A HANDSOME THIN MAN APPEARS
    A NICK FOR A NORA
    FOR WHOM WE MIGHT POUR A FEW

DASHIELL HAMMETT:
    QUITE A FEW

BARTENDERS:
    A CATCH OF A CATCH, SUCH A COUP

DASHIELL HAMMETT:
    WE SPOKE

DASHIELL HAMMETT AND LILLIAN:
    WE DRANK, WE KNEW

BARTENDER: The usual, Mr. Hammett?

DASHIELL HAMMETT: *[Quoting lines from* The Thin Man.*]* "You know, Vic, the important thing is rhythm. You always have rhythm in your shaking. A Manhattan you shake to a fox-trot. A Rob Roy you shake to two-step time. A dry martini you always shake to waltz time." *[To* LILLIAN.*]* Say, how many drinks have you had?

LILLIAN: This will make five martinis.

DASHIELL HAMMETT: All right, will you bring me four more martinis, Leo? Line them up right here. *[*DASHIELL HAMMETT *starts to drink the martinis, one by one.]*

LILLIAN: After he wrote *The Thin Man,* he told me I was Nora, and I was very pleased, and then he told me I was also the silly girl in it, and the villainess, too. And he wrote me poetry, and he was so handsome, and he called me "My darling Lilishka." Didn't you, Dash? Dash?

DASHIELL HAMMETT, *apparently drunk, falls off the bar stool onto the floor.*

I met Hammett—Dashiell Hammett—in Musso and Frank's Restaurant in Los Angeles in 1930. He'd written *The Maltese Falcon* and *The Dain Curse*. He was the hottest thing in town. When I met Hammett, I was a reader at MGM and didn't have a political bone in my body or a nickel to my name. When he got done with me, I was Lillian Hellman.

On-screen we see the scene from Julia *in which Jane Fonda, playing* LILLIAN, *is living with Jason Robards, playing* DASHIELL HAMMETT. *She's trying to write. She types a few words on a piece of paper and then crumples it up. She tries again and crumples another piece of paper. Then she throws the typewriter out the window.*

That never happened.

MARY: Thank you. Almost none of it happened. Hammett—you and Hammett—you rarely slept together, he was drunk most of the time, and he had the longest writer's block in living memory.

LILLIAN: He loved me and only me.

MARY: I'm sure he did. But this romantic thin man who rode into your life and turned you into a femme fatale was a figment of your imagination. He was just a story.

LILLIAN: If you want to believe that, it makes no difference to me. Because you don't know the first thing about stories. If you did, you wouldn't do silly things like telling us there are no nightingales in North America. Fine, Hammett was just a story. And one day he gave me a book of British court cases and said, "Here's something." In it was an article about a girls' school in Scotland where two headmistresses were accused by a student of having a lesbian relationship. The scandal forced the school to close, and the headmistresses sued the student for libel. I was very lucky, because he'd given me something that had structure, it had a subject—

MARY: Its subject was lying—

LILLIAN: I called the play *The Children's Hour,* and it was, for its time, shocking. It's always nice to begin with something shocking. It's a way of saying—*[A little Mae West.]* "I'm here. Notice me, boys. Come over to my corner of the playground and I'll show you my underpants." I was a sensation, and I was twenty-nine.

The BARTENDERS *shake up a new round of drinks, and a man in a top hat enters and sits down next to* MARY. *He is high-waisted and slightly overweight. This is* EDMUND WILSON.

MARY:

WE SPOKE, WE DRANK, WE KNEW—

BARTENDERS:

EDMUND WILSON APPEARS—

MARY:

THE SCENT OF DISASTER
THE CLINK OF A GLASS AND YOU

BARTENDERS:

> HE WAS OLD HE WAS NEW

MARY:

> A VOICE LIKE MY OWN SAID "I DO"
> I WOKE, I SANK, I FLEW

For many years—for most of my life, really—I tried to figure out why I married Edmund Wilson. He was, of course, brilliant. Say something brilliant, Edmund.

EDMUND WILSON: Something brilliant.

MARY: And he was famous for being a great deal of fun. Say something fun, Edmund.

EDMUND WILSON: Something fun.

MARY: And he was eminent. And clever. And he was interested in all sorts of odd things. Puppets. He could take a bow tie and turn it into a tiny mouse—

He turns a bow tie into a tiny mouse.

EDMUND WILSON: Squeak squeak.

MARY: —and he had met Harry Houdini, and he could do magic tricks.

EDMUND WILSON *stands and removes his top hat and pulls a rabbit out of it. He exits with the rabbit.*

He was called Bunny, but not because of the rabbit. *[Indicating* LILLIAN.*] She* loved him.

LILLIAN: I did. I didn't really know him until years later, but I absolutely adored him. Everyone did.

BARTENDERS:

EVERYONE LOVED HIM

AND NOBODY SHOVED HIM DOWN ANYONE'S THROAT

MARY:

THIS IS TRUE

BARTENDERS:

AND MAY WE NOTE THAT WE KNEW

AND ADORED HIM

LILLIAN: Everyone did. Everyone but you.

MARY: Did you ever—?

LILLIAN: Sleep with Edmund Wilson? Absolutely not. Although I did sleep with Philip Rahv. Once.

BARTENDERS:

SHE SLEPT WITH PHILIP RAHV

MARY: Not even once. *[Beat.]* I was sleeping with Philip Rahv when I met Edmund Wilson. I was in love with Philip Rahv.

LILLIAN: No one remembers Philip Rahv. They all think you're talking about Philip Roth. *[To the audience.]* It's Philip *Rahv—[She mouths the words, "And I did sleep with him."]*

MARY: Philip Rahv was tall and handsome and about to become the editor of *Partisan Review*—and I was just starting to write criticism. We lived together in a one-room apartment, and we argued endlessly about everything. Whether Jews were superior to gentiles—which he believed, of course. It was as if he were on a game show—

PHILIP RAHV *enters, pushing a small table.*

Jewish geniuses for five hundred dollars.

PHILIP RAHV: *[A slight Russian accent.]* Einstein, Marx, Spinoza—

MARY: Exactly. He was very intense. We waged class struggle every day.

LILLIAN: "My First Jew" by Mary McCarthy.

BARTENDERS:
    A SMOKE, A DRINK, A JEW
    A WAR OF THE CLASSES
    A MURKY MORASS FOR TWO

PHILIP RAHV:
    I LOVE THE STRUGGLE OF THE MASSES WITH YOU

BARTENDERS:
    THOSE CIRCULAR FIGHTS WE'D PURSUE

MARY *walks over to the table, which is set for dinner, and starts to cut a loaf of bread.*

PHILIP RAHV: Marcel Proust, Franz Kafka—

MARY: I'm not playing this game with you anymore—

PHILIP RAHV: Because you always lose.

MARY: I do not always lose. How can I lose with Shakespeare on
my team?

PHILIP RAHV: But Sigmund Freud is not on your team—

MARY: I'm not playing, Philip—

PHILIP RAHV: Or Jascha Heifetz, or Vladimir Horowitz—

MARY *takes a particularly vicious cut at the loaf of bread.*

LILLIAN:
A SMOKE

MARY:
A DRINK

PHILIP RAHV:
A JEW

A beat.

What are you doing?

MARY: I'm cutting the crusts off.

PHILIP RAHV: Do you know why you're cutting the crusts off?

MARY: Because the sandwich tastes better with the crusts off—

PHILIP RAHV *shakes his head—that's not the right answer.*

Because I grew up in a family where they cut the crusts off—

Wrong answer again.

I give up.

PHILIP RAHV: The reason people cut the crusts off bread is so they can throw the crusts away. Which shows the world that they have money, so much money they don't even need the whole piece of bread. It's a way for the middle-class goyim to pretend to be upper-class goyim—

MARY: *[Interrupting.]* It makes the sandwiches look nicer.

PHILIP RAHV: It's very bourgeois.

MARY: Liking pretty things doesn't make you bourgeois.

PHILIP RAHV: Caring about them does.

He stands and picks up a pretty little vase with a few flowers in it.

MARY: What are you doing?

PHILIP RAHV: Watch this—

He starts across the room toward MARY *and lets the vase fly out of his hand—*MARY *screams.*

MARY: Philip!—

He catches the vase.

PHILIP RAHV: It's just a possession. Possessions mean nothing.

MARY: It was my grandmother's. It's practically all I have from my grandmother.

PHILIP RAHV: It's a thing. It's just a thing. Who needs it?

MARY: What would you suggest I put flowers in?

PHILIP RAHV: Where is it written we have to have flowers?

MARY: Oh, I suppose there's a Marxist position on flowers—

PHILIP RAHV: And as for linen napkins—

He holds up a linen napkin.

MARY: They were my grandmother's—

He picks up a silver fork.

PHILIP RAHV: And silver—

He puts the fork back as MARY *says:*

MARY: The silver was—

PHILIP AND MARY: *[Together.]* My grandmother's.

PHILIP RAHV: You know what my grandmother left me? A scrap of paper. And you know what was on that scrap of paper? A message. And you know what that message said? "When the Cossacks come, don't open the door."

A beat.

MARY: I suppose Jews don't care about things they own—

PHILIP RAHV: Oh, voila. Now it comes out—

MARY: *[With a much better French accent.]* It's "voila."

PHILIP RAHV: *[Fracturing the pronunciation.]* Voila yourself. *[A beat.]*

MARY: *[Repeating his line.]* Voila now *what* comes out?

PHILIP RAHV: Voila, scratch a goy and you find an anti-Semite.

MARY: I am not an anti-Semite. That is so ludicrous. It's all right for you to accuse me of being overly attached to meaningless objects, but when I suggest that *your* people are not exactly—

PHILIP RAHV: *My* people. Oy, oy, oy, that's good. My people are not exactly what? Say it, go on—

MARY: Your people—some of your people—some of your people living on Park Avenue, for instance—are not exactly living on bread and water—

PHILIP RAHV: But if they were, they would eat the crusts. *[He stands.]* Good-bye. I'm going into the bathroom to stare at my foreskin.

MARY: You don't have a foreskin.

PHILIP RAHV: Exactly.

PHILIP RAHV *goes into the bathroom and slams the door. A beat.*

MARY: We were incredibly happy. *[She goes to the bureau and takes out a fox stole and wraps it around her neck. Re: the stole.]* My grandmother's. *[Beat.]* One day Philip had a lunch for the great critic Edmund Wilson and took me to it. I wore my best black dress and a silver fox stole. He— Edmund—was short and stout and pink and pop-eyed, and he huffed and he puffed all the way through lunch. A few weeks later he took me to dinner. Here's what I had for dinner: three daiquiris, two double Manhattans, a bottle of red wine, and several tumblers of B&B. Two weeks later a similar dinner, and then to his house in Connecticut. I was shown to a guest bedroom. I decided to come down to the study where I knew he would be. It was late. There was a couch. He misunderstood why I had come, and took me in his arms, and I gave up the battle.

BARTENDERS:
A COUCH, A KISS, AND YOU
THE RAPTUROUS FORCE
OF A FUTURE DIVORCE
FOR TWO
BEFORE IT BEGAN
IT WAS THROUGH

LILLIAN: You slept with him because you were drunk.

MARY: That wasn't the reason—

LILLIAN: Why are you making this into the turning point of the twentieth century?

MARY: But I didn't come down to the study to sleep with him. And I tried to explain that to him later. Not that he cared—the only thing he cared about was that it had happened. I'd slept with him, that was the fact, case closed. But I hadn't gone there to sleep with him. I'd gone there to talk to him, I swear, I'd gone there only to talk to him.

LILLIAN: Listen to this, you wrote this: "She married him as a punishment for the sin of having slept with him when she did not love him, when she loved . . . someone else."

MARY: I also wrote, "It made no sense for me to sleep with him, so I married him so it would make sense."

LILLIAN: Bullshit. What about ambition? What about vanity? What about how pleased you had to have been that this brilliant man had chosen you? Or did you think it was only because you were "a princess among the trolls"?

MARY: I didn't write that about *myself*. I wrote it about a character in a short story.

LILLIAN: [*Dismissively.*] It was fiction. Hmmph.

MARY: Yes. It was.

LILLIAN: You wrote fact and called it fiction—

MARY: And you wrote fiction and called it fact.

LILLIAN: Ooh ooh ooh, that is so painful.

MARY: Was there ever a moment we could have been friends?

LILLIAN: Hard to imagine.

They both think about it for a moment.

When would it have been?

MARY: Hard to imagine. *[Beat.]* But isn't it odd? The two of us might never have become real writers if it weren't for these two older men who came into our lives at almost the same moment. After we were married, Edmund led me to a small guest bedroom on the ground floor of his house. There was a desk and a typewriter. He put me in that room and closed the door, and I became a writer. I wrote short stories, and they were published, and one of them was called "The Man in the Brooks Brothers Shirt." It was about a young woman who meets a traveling salesman on a train, and they get drunk, and she wakes up naked in his sleeping berth. It was very shocking, it was, it was shocking, and because of it, I was a sensation, and I was twenty-nine.

LILLIAN: *[Mae West again.]* "Hey, boys, come on over and I'll show you my underpants."

MARY: Literally. In the story was a pair of underpants.

LILLIAN: With a safety pin in them.

MARY: You read it?

LILLIAN: Of course I read it. Everyone read it.

MARY: Did you like it?

LILLIAN: Did I like it? After all those horrible things you said about me and my work?

MARY: I was just wondering what you thought of it.

LILLIAN: I liked it. I liked *Memories of a Catholic Girlhood,* too.

MARY: Thank you. I liked *The Children's Hour.*

LILLIAN *looks at her, surprised.*

Your plays were so well made. Too well made, really—there was way too much of the gun over the mantel in the first act being fired at the end of the play—

LILLIAN: Let's just go back to you liked it.

BARTENDERS:
THEY CLASH, THEY LINK

MARY: I did.

LILLIAN: Thank you.

BARTENDERS:
INCENSED IN SYNC

Both women start to say something, then change their minds.

A SMOKE, A DRINK

LILLIAN AND MARY:
AND YOU

MARY AND LILLIAN: *[To a* BARTENDER.*]* Bartender!

BLACKOUT.

Scene 4

Reds.

A huge red parachute silk curtain drops from the flies.

ENSEMBLE:
    ARE YOU NOW
    HAVE YOU EVER
    STATE YOUR NAME
    DO YOU SWEAR
    GIVE US NAMES
    WHO WAS THERE
    WAS THERE ANYBODY ELSE
    IT'S THE HOUSE
    UN-AMERICAN
    HAVE YOU EVER BEEN
    DID YOU KNOW
    WERE YOU THERE
    I REFUSE ON THE GROUND
    GIVE US NAMES
    DO YOU SWEAR
    ARE YOU NOW
    DID YOU EVER

THE COMMITTEE IS IN ORDER
GIVE US NAMES
ARE YOU NOW
HAVE YOU EVER EVER BEEN
STATE YOUR NAME
SO HELP YOU GOD

We see LILLIAN *and* MARY *dressed as young women.*

ANNOUNCER: Are you now or have you ever been a member of the—

MARY: Me? Are you serious? I was the palest of pinkos. I marched in the May Day parade in my prettiest dress. I became a Trotskyite almost by chance—

LILLIAN: No one here even knows what a Trotskyite is anymore—

MARY: No one here knows what a Stalinist is, either. She was a Stalinist. Tell them what you believed—

LILLIAN: I never said I was a Stalinist.

MARY: You're dead. Tell them. What can happen?

LILLIAN *isn't going to admit it.*

All right, then: had you been a Stalinist, what might you have believed?

LILLIAN: The Stalinists believed that a certain amount of bad stuff was part of any revolution, and that it would eventually stop.

MARY: And the Trotskyites believed that bad stuff was bad stuff and would lead to more bad stuff.

LILLIAN: The Stalinists turned out to be wrong.

MARY: So wrong. So very very wrong.

LILLIAN: I said they were wrong.

MARY: And we turned out to be right. *[Beat.]* Anyway, how I became a Trotskyite. It was 1936, I was living in New York, and everyone in New York was a leftist. I would never have made a true Marxist—it's something you have to take up early, like ballet—but then the Moscow trials began. Leon Trotsky, one of the leaders of the Russian revolution, was accused of being a traitor, and thousands of people were sent to Siberia or executed for being in cahoots with him. It was a monstrous frame-up engineered by Joseph Stalin, it was completely unjust, but the truth is that when it began, I didn't know a thing about it because I was off in Reno, getting a divorce from my first husband. When I got back—

We hear the sound of argument and see a Village party. There's a table with bottles and paper cups and a group of men intensely talking. One of them is JAMES T. FARRELL.

JAMES T. FARRELL: You can't mean it—

MARY: That's James T. Farrell, who wrote *Studs Lonigan*—

JAMES T. FARRELL: You can't possibly read what Trotsky wrote and think there's any way he collaborated with the Germans—

All the following partygoer dialogue is meant to overlap.

PARTYGOER #1: But Holtzman testified he met with Trotsky at the Hotel Bristol in Copenhagen—

PARTYGOER #2: But the Hotel Bristol in Copenhagen burned to the ground in 1912—

PARTYGOER #3: So they couldn't possibly have met at the Hotel Bristol—

JAMES T. FARRELL: He's being framed and he deserves a hearing. Surely he deserves a hearing. Mary thinks so, don't you, dear?

MARY: [To the audience.] I had no idea what they were talking about. [To JAMES T. FARRELL.] Come again?

JAMES T. FARRELL: Trotsky—

MARY: Trotsky—

JAMES T. FARRELL: Deserves a hearing. Don't you think?

MARY: Has something happened to Trotsky?

JAMES T. FARRELL: Has something happened to Trotsky? She wants to know if something has happened to Trotsky—

MARY: I'm sorry.

JAMES T. FARRELL: Trotsky's been falsely accused of plotting with the Nazis to murder almost everyone in the Kremlin. Sixteen Bolsheviks have implicated him, and they've all been executed. Trotsky denies the charges. So he deserves a hearing, right?

MARY: [*To the audience re:* JAMES T. FARRELL.] I liked him so much. [*To* JAMES T. FARRELL.] Yes. A hearing. Absolutely. Everyone deserves a hearing.

JAMES T. FARRELL: Not to mention asylum, don't you think?

MARY: [*Once again this is a surprise, but she's trying to bluff her way through as best she can.*] Asylum. Great idea.

She and JAMES T. FARRELL *toast.* MARY *walks away from the party.*

A few days later I opened the mail and found a letter from a group that was demanding Trotsky's right to a hearing and to asylum, and my name was on the letterhead. No one had even asked me. They had no right. So I decided to remove my name from the list that very minute. And I meant to. Truly I did. But I forgot. And then, after a day or two, the phone rang. It was a Stalinist I barely knew, calling to persuade me to resign from this committee I hadn't even joined. I hung up, and the phone rang again, and again. "You must withdraw." "There will be consequences." "Think it over, Mary." It made me very angry. So I never took my name off the list. And—[*Shrugs.*] that's how I became a Trotskyite. I became a fanatic Trotskyite. I signed letters, I marched, I slept only with other Trotskyites—with a few exceptions—and I went to meetings where I was shouted down and accused of being the sort of person who "looked for pimples on the great smiling face of the Soviet Union."

LILLIAN: So you were an accidental Trotskyite, just as you were an accidental Mrs. Edmund Wilson. Just out of curiosity, what decisions in your life did you actually make?

MARY: What I believe is that the decisions we agonize over are often the most insignificant—what to have for dinner, beef or chicken. What color to make the rug. But the big things almost seem to choose you. I was like "Stendhal's hero, who took part in something confused and disarrayed that he later learned was the Battle of Waterloo." I had no idea that I was making the most important decision of my life—to be serious, to be involved with public affairs, to be an intellectual. And I had no idea that I was choosing not just to be a Trotskyite but to be an anti-communist. Of course, I wasn't a right-wing anti-communist like Senator McCarthy, I was a liberal, you understand the distinction—

LILLIAN: Well, I don't, as you know. I don't understand that at all. Are you done?

MARY *waves to* LILLIAN *to proceed.*

I don't have a little story that makes my politics make sense. But there was nothing whimsical about my ending up where I did, even though it's hard to be explicit about why. But I suppose—growing up in the South, seeing the way blacks were treated—well, that's probably too simple. . . . Once I was with Sophronia, and I refused to sit in the back of the bus. The driver threw us off, and Sophronia was very angry with me, because she thought I was showing off. . . .

MARY: Ladies and gentlemen, Miss Rosa Parks—

LILLIAN: When I got older and realized I probably would never make much of a radical, I was nonetheless attracted to them. And then I got involved with Hammett, who *was* committed, no question, and we all hated the Nazis and we all cared

about the workers. . . . *[Beat.]* Too simple, too simple. . . .
And guilt, guilt played a part. Because I was successful during the Depression. . . . *[Beat.]* And, of course, I'd gone to Rus-
sia before the war, and it was hard to go there and not have
feelings for the Russian people. They were our allies at the
time. I wanted the revolution to work. Sue me. *[Beat.]* And I
had a kind of impatience with . . . splitting hairs . . . with
people who were always finding ways to get around believing
in something, people who were looking for loopholes—

MARY: Finding pimples—

LILLIAN: Seizing on technicalities and using them as an excuse to
avoid taking a position on something that was worth taking
a position on. Which side are you on, boys, which side are
you on. I didn't want to be on your side, quibbling—it
seemed like quibbling—I wanted—

MARY: —to be one of the boys.

LILLIAN: We all wanted to be one of the boys.

MARY: I never wanted to be one of the boys—

LILLIAN: But you wanted to be the only woman at the table,
which is practically the same thing. I wanted to be brave. I
wanted to be on the side of change and equality—

MARY: *We* were for change and equality—

LILLIAN: But it didn't feel that way. It felt as if you were just a
bunch of critics. Being against things was easy. I wanted to
be *for* something. That was the hard part.

MARY: So you overlooked "the bad stuff." The technicalities. The purges, the murders, the Nazi-Soviet Pact—how could you have remained sympathetic after the Nazi-Soviet Pact?

LILLIAN: Miss Hellman does not wish to discuss the Nazi-Soviet Pact—

MARY: I know. And you never did. You just said, "We were wrong," as if that was that, as if that took care of the fact that you looked the other way when it was all staring you in the face—

LILLIAN: You're just angry because we became heroes—

MARY: What?

LILLIAN: Think about it. It's true. The war ended, the Russians were no longer our allies, I was blacklisted, thousands of people were blacklisted. And all of you—all of you who were so "right" about things didn't lift a finger to help. And then the House Un-American Activities Committee came along and gave us all a chance to do something brave. [Beat.] And I went there on that bad morning—

MARY: In your Balmain dress—

LILLIAN: Yes. In my Balmain dress and a brand-new hat and a beautiful pair of white kid gloves. I was fabulous.

MARY: And lest anyone forget, she wrote an entire book about it. You'd have thought the woman had gone to jail. Years later there was a play on Broadway—the testimony of the people who'd appeared before the committee, all of it in the public record, and of course her statement was read, it was the high point of the play, and she actually asked to be paid for it.

LILLIAN: I did. And guess what? They paid me!

She laughs. MARY *laughs, too. A knock at the door.* LILLIAN *stands and goes over to a door. She opens it. A* SUMMONS SERVER *is there.*

SUMMONS SERVER: Are you Lillian Hellman?

LILLIAN: Yes?

He hands her a subpoena. LILLIAN *opens the envelope. Then she puts on her hat and her white kid gloves.*

ENSEMBLE:
    GIVE US NAMES
    DO YOU SWEAR
    ARE YOU NOW
    DID YOU EVER
    THE COMMITTEE IS IN ORDER
    GIVE US NAMES
    ARE YOU NOW
    HAVE YOU EVER EVER BEEN
    STATE YOUR NAME
    SO HELP YOU GOD

ANNOUNCER: Are you now or have you ever been a member of the Communist Party?

LILLIAN: *[From her letter to the committee.]* "I am not willing, now or in the future, to bring bad trouble to people who, in my past association with them, were completely innocent of any talk or any action that was disloyal or sub-versive. . . . To hurt innocent people whom I knew many years ago in order to save myself is, to me, inhuman and indecent and dishonorable. I cannot and will not cut my conscience to fit this year's fashions, even though I long ago came to the conclusion that I was not a political person and could have no comfortable place in any political group. . . . I would, therefore, like to come before you and speak of myself. I am prepared to tell you anything you wish to know about my views or actions if your Committee will agree to refrain from asking me to name other people. If the Committee is unwilling to give me this assurance, I will be forced to plead the privilege of the Fifth Amendment at this hearing."

MARY *yanks at the red parachute drop, and it vanishes.*

Scene 5

What happened at Sarah Lawrence.

MARY *emerges from the wings, pulling a rope that brings a porch onto the stage.*

LILLIAN: What's this?

MARY: Sarah Lawrence College. You skipped right over it.

LILLIAN: It wasn't that important.

MARY: It's where we met.

LILLIAN: *[Referring to her letter to the committee.]* As far as I'm concerned, that was the first-act curtain.

MARY: But first Sarah Lawrence. It's 1948.

LILLIAN: I suppose I have to get the tea.

MARY: I got the porch.

> LILLIAN *goes offstage and returns pushing a table with a large silver tea service of cups and saucers.* MARY *arranges the women in the* ENSEMBLE. *She calls in* HAROLD TAYLOR *and places him to the right of* LILLIAN's *chair.*

LILLIAN: There were many more people than this.

MARY: We don't have many more people.

LILLIAN: Well, then use some of the men to fill in.

> *Some of the men in the* ENSEMBLE *sit with the women.*

Where was I?

MARY: Over there.

> LILLIAN *walks to her chair.*

Are you ready?

LILLIAN: Are you ready?

MARY: All right. Stephen Spender invited us to speak—

LILLIAN: I don't think so. Harold Taylor, the president of Sarah Lawrence, invited us to speak. Not that it matters.

MARY: You're talking to the students when I come in. Stephen is there.

STEPHEN SPENDER *waves hello.*

You're out on the sunporch at the president's house—

STEPHEN SPENDER: No, no, that's not right—

MARY *and* LILLIAN *look at* STEPHEN SPENDER.

It wasn't at the president's house—

MARY: Where was it, then?

STEPHEN SPENDER: It was at *my* house—

MARY: On Stephen Spender's sunporch, then—

STEPHEN SPENDER: We didn't have a sunporch.

MARY: It was definitely on a sunporch. So it must have been at the president's house—

STEPHEN SPENDER: I'm positive it was at my house—

LILLIAN *stands.*

LILLIAN: Never mind. What am I saying?

MARY: You're talking about John Dos Passos.

As LILLIAN *sits back down:*

LILLIAN: You have to explain who John Dos Passos is—

STEPHEN SPENDER: *[By way of explanation.]* A famous novelist and radical—

MARY: You were saying that John Dos Passos had gone to Spain during the Spanish civil war and turned against the loyalist cause because he didn't like the food in Madrid. And you didn't notice me, probably because I looked quite young at the time. I couldn't bear it. All those lies, so smooth, as if they were coming out of a tube. And you were so clever. You weren't being hostile at all. "Oh, that Dos," you were saying—

LILLIAN: *[Repeating.]* "Oh, that Dos." Like that?

MARY: Just like that. "He did love his food."

LILLIAN: *[Repeating.]* "He did love his food."

MARY: Is it coming back to you?

LILLIAN: No. It doesn't sound like me at all.

MARY: And I interrupted. And I said— *[To the* STUDENTS, *heatedly.]* "John Dos Passos didn't turn against the loyalists, he turned against the communists. And it wasn't because of the food in Madrid—it was because one of his closest friends in Spain, an incredibly brave man named Andres Nin, had just

been tortured and murdered in a communist prison by Stalinists, that's why." *[She has moved herself to tears.]*

LILLIAN: Were you actually crying?

MARY: I was very upset. And then you jangled the bracelets—

MARY *signals for the bracelets to descend. They do.* LILLIAN
looks up to see them.

LILLIAN: But I never wore bracelets.

MARY: Of course you wore bracelets.

LILLIAN: You must have me confused with someone else.

MARY: There are pictures of you wearing bracelets—

LILLIAN: Nonsense. Get those goddamn bracelets out of here.
[They vanish.]

STEPHEN SPENDER: *[Thinking it over.]* I'm starting to wonder if I
was even there—

MARY: Of course you were there—

LILLIAN: Maybe he wasn't—

STEPHEN SPENDER: *[To* MARY.*]* I do remember that afterwards
she said we'd arranged the entire episode so we could red-
bait her.

MARY: Well, how could we have red-baited her? How could we
have arranged for her to say something so perfectly idiotic?

LILLIAN: Are you the only person who's allowed to say that people sometimes do serious things for shallow reasons?

MARY: But in his case, it wasn't true.

LILLIAN: How do you know? How do we know why anyone does anything? In real life, I mean.

STEPHEN SPENDER: If I could just throw something in here that is only going to confuse things, I'm afraid. A few months earlier, before any of this happened, I had dinner with John Dos Passos. He had been in England, which had just elected a socialist government, and he announced that he no longer believed in socialism because he'd gone to a restaurant in London and found a bug in his chicken.

A beat.

LILLIAN: A bad moment for your team.

MARY: Thank you, Stephen. Thank you for that.

STEPHEN SPENDER: It doesn't mean your version isn't accurate—

MARY: It's not "my version." It's what happened.

LILLIAN: It's not what happened.

STEPHEN SPENDER: What do *you* think happened?

LILLIAN: What do I think happened? I thought you'd never ask. *[She stands and moves some of the furniture around.]* I was here. *[She sits down.]* Harold—you're next to me.

And the sunlight was coming into the room, like so—*[A light hits her.]* Even more sunlight. *[The light gets a little brighter.]* Lovely. And the students were sitting on the floor, because so many of them had turned up to see me that there weren't enough chairs—

The STUDENTS *sit on the floor.*

They sat cross-legged, looking up at me like little fish—no, like baby birds in a nest, waiting to be fed—*[She motions to the* STUDENTS *to tilt their chins upward slightly.]* When I suddenly noticed—over there—

She motions to MARY *to move to the other side of the room.* MARY *crosses and the* STUDENTS *turn to watch her.*

The students never took their eyes off me—

The STUDENTS *turn back to* LILLIAN.

—a quivering dark cylinder of rage. *[To the lighting person.]* Even darker. *[The light on* MARY *dims.]* She was holding a teacup and saucer—

MARY *is handed a teacup and saucer, or perhaps a teacup and saucer are lowered from the ceiling on a hook.*

I was talking. I'd been asked a question—

A STUDENT *raises her hand.*

STUDENT: Did you ever meet Ernest Hemingway?

LILLIAN: "Did I ever meet Ernest Hemingway?" And I was answering. I was saying . . . *[To the* STUDENTS.*]* I would have starved to death in Spain but for Ernest. Because when I told him I was going there, during the war, he said to me, "Bring food, there's none." And when he and I had dinner in Madrid, in someone's apartment, I brought sardines and pâté. And Ernest said thank God I had, because Dos Passos had just been there and hadn't brought any food at all and ended up eating everyone else's. That's what I said, it was completely harmless, and Madam over there began shaking—you could hear her teacup rattling against the saucer. *[To* MARY.*]* Go ahead. I did your version. Do mine.

MARY *starts shaking her teacup against her saucer.*

And she said—

MARY: How can you say that about Dos?

LILLIAN: *Dos.* So she would be sure I would know she knew him. "How can you say that about Dos?" What had I said? And perhaps I said something like "Well, Dos loved his food," and she reacted quite bizarrely. She said—

MARY: *[Shaking her cup and saucer.]* You're just saying that because you can't stand that he went over to the other side—

LILLIAN: Good. Keep shaking the cup.

MARY: You're just saying that because you've never admitted what the Stalinists did in Spain—*[*MARY *continues, overlapping with* LILLIAN.*]*

LILLIAN: I had no idea what was going on. I turned to the president of the school and said—*[Turning to one of the people in the room.]* "Who is that girl?" And he said—

PRESIDENT: Mary McCarthy.

LILLIAN: And I said "Oh." I said, "Oh, the one who married Edmund Wilson for his looks." And some of the students laughed—the ones who knew what Edmund Wilson looked like—

Many of the students laugh. So does LILLIAN.

And she dropped her cup and saucer on the floor—

MARY: What?

LILLIAN: And they shattered into a million tiny pieces.

MARY: Never happened—

LILLIAN: Go ahead, do it—

MARY *drops the teacup and saucer on the floor, and they break into tiny pieces.*

And Harold Taylor's maid came rushing in to sweep it up.

MARY: I knew a black maid would enter the scene. *[To the audience.]* She could never write a play that didn't have a black maid in it, speaking in the most appalling way—

BLACK MAID: Lawd, Lawd, Lawd, it ain't right to let young'uns use the good china, Mistah Taylor. Ah tol' you this would happen—

LILLIAN: Actually, the maid said nothing.

MARY: Well, had she spoken, that's the sort of thing you would have had her say.

STEPHEN SPENDER: I don't remember any of this. Where was I?

LILLIAN: You weren't there, Stephen. We went to your house *afterwards. [To* MARY.] You came to pick a fight. Why? Was it because I slept with Philip Rahv?

MARY: You never slept with Philip Rahv—

LILLIAN: Fine. Scratch Philip Rahv as a possible explanation. Were you jealous of me?

MARY: *[Incredulous.]* Jealous? Of what?

LILLIAN: I know. What can it be? Not my looks, certainly. So: my money? My fame? My farm!? Tell the truth, you always wanted a farm—

MARY: I am not a jealous person.

LILLIAN: Nor am I.

MARY: It's just too easy to say that the reason women fight with each other is because they're jealous.

LILLIAN: Absolutely. We had plenty of reasons to dislike each other. Good reasons.

MARY: Real reasons. I'm just not a jealous person.

LILLIAN: Hmmmph.

MARY: Although I have to say I have never known a jealous person who admitted to being a jealous person.

LILLIAN: Neither have I. *[They nod. A small moment between them, perhaps.]*

STEPHEN SPENDER: *[Trying to find some common ground.]* So are we in agreement about something?

MARY: We are.

LILLIAN: We had a fight.

MARY: Exactly.

LILLIAN: And you dined out on it for years—

MARY: *You* dined out on it for years—

LILLIAN: *[Imitating MARY.]* "I was so young, she thought I was a student"—

MARY: "They came there to red-bait me"—

LILLIAN: "Dos"—

MARY: "Ernest"—

LILLIAN: Was there ever a moment we could have been friends?

MARY: Friends? Hard to imagine.

STEPHEN SPENDER: Ladies! Ladies!

MARY: We had a fight.

LILLIAN: A skirmish, really.

MARY: And the captain of the first U-boat straightened her stockings and drove back to her home.

LILLIAN: And the captain of the second U-boat straightened her stockings and drove back to her farm. Which *was* a farm.

A woman enters from the wings. This is MURIEL GARDINER.

MURIEL GARDINER: Oh. Am I in the right place?

MARY: Hello. You're early. I didn't expect you for an hour—

MURIEL GARDINER: I know. I had a cancellation and nowhere else to go, really—

LILLIAN *looks at* MURIEL GARDINER, *curious.*

LILLIAN: Who is this person?

MARY: Have you ever seen her before?

LILLIAN: Never.

MARY: This person is the gun over the mantel.

MURIEL GARDINER: Bang.

MARY: Not yet.

BLACKOUT.

CURTAIN.

ACT 2

Scene 1

MARY *and* LILLIAN *come onstage carrying their dolls and sit on the edge of the stage. Behind them is the fig tree and* MARY'S *house.* MARY *begins to sing "Imaginary Friend."*

MARY: *[To her doll.]*
    I BELONG TO YOU
    YOU BELONG TO ME
    YOU PLAY MY FAV'RITE GAMES
    NEVER CALL ME NAMES
    NEVER DISAGREE
    ALL THAT LONELY LONELINESS IS THROUGH
    WITH AN IMAGINARY FRIEND
    LIKE YOU

LILLIAN: *[To her doll.]*
    WHAT WAS THAT YOU SAID?
    YOU SAY THE SWEETEST THINGS
    YOU ALWAYS MAKE ME BLUSH
    WITH THE KINDA MUSH
    YOUR DEVOTION BRINGS
    CLOSE AS "A" WILL ALWAYS BE TO "B"
    THAT'S MY IMAGINARY FRIEND
    AND ME

LILLIAN AND MARY: *[To their dolls.]*
>DANCIN' WITH MY DOLLY DOWN A COUNTRY LANE
>YOU'RE JUST PLAIN TRUE BLUE
>SWEETER THAN THE CANDY OF A CANDY CANE
>YOU REMAIN
>IMAGINARY

MARY: *[To her doll.]*
>I BELIEVE IN YOU

LILLIAN: *[To her doll.]*
>I BELIEVE IN YOU

MARY:
>YOU BELIEVE IN ME

LILLIAN:
>YOU BELIEVE IN ME

LILLIAN AND MARY:
>NICE OF YOU TO COME
>YOU'LL BE TWEEDLEDUM
>I'LL BE TWEEDLEDEE
>WHEN I HAVE A THOUGHT, YOU'LL HAVE IT, TOO
>YOU'RE MY IMAGINARY FRIEND
>'MAGINARY FRIEND
>LET IT NEVER END
>LET IT NEVER END
>'CAUSE I CAN DEPEND
>YES I CAN DEPEND
>ON—

DOLLS:
>ON ME

WHEN WE GO OUT AND PLAY

LILLIAN AND MARY:
WHEN WE GO OUT AND PLAY

DOLLS:
YOU'RE ALWAYS ON MY SIDE

LILLIAN AND MARY:
ALWAYS ON MY SIDE

DOLLS:
YOU NEVER LET ME DOWN
NEVER SIT AND FROWN
NEVER MISS A STRIDE

LILLIAN AND MARY:
WITH ME STRIDE FOR STRIDE

DOLLS:
WHAT'S MORE FUN THAN MONKEYS IN THE ZOO?

LILLIAN AND MARY:
IT'S AN IMAGINARY FRIEND

ALL FOUR:
OR TWO
DANCIN' WITH MY DOLLY DOWN A COUNTRY LANE
CLOUDS AND RAIN WON'T DO

LILLIAN AND MARY:
WAITIN' FOR MY DADDY AT THE CHOO-CHOO TRAIN

ALL FOUR:

>WE REMAIN
>
>WE REMAIN
>
>SO VERY MERRY
>
>I BELONG TO YOU
>
>YOU BELONG TO ME
>
>SWEETER THAN A YAM
>
>OR A JAR O' JAM
>
>AT A JAMBOREE
>
>ICKY-WICKY THOUGHTS GO WICKY WOO
>
>WITH AN IMAGINARY FRIEND
>
>'MAGINARY FRIEND
>
>LET IT NEVER END
>
>LET IT NEVER END
>
>'CAUSE I CAN DEPEND
>
>YES I CAN DEPEND
>
>YES I CAN DEPEND
>
>UPON A FRIEND
>
>IT'LL NEVER END
>
>NOT WITH AN IMAGINARY FRIEND
>
>LIKE YOU

MARY *sits on the porch steps.* UNCLE MYERS *emerges from the house. He takes out a razor strop and flicks it against the porch railing with a sharp snap.*

UNCLE MYERS: Mary—

MARY: Yes, Uncle—

UNCLE MYERS: I gave your brother a tin butterfly several days ago.

MARY: I know. From a Cracker Jack box. Will you get me one? Please? I would love one so much.

UNCLE MYERS: He can't find it. Have you seen it anywhere?

MARY: No. So it's lost?

UNCLE MYERS: Well, that all depends, doesn't it. . . .

UNCLE MYERS *flicks his strop against the railing again. Then he walks into the house. A beat.* UNCLE MYERS *comes back out of the house with the strop.*

Mary—

MARY: Yes, Uncle—

UNCLE MYERS: Are you sure you haven't seen the butterfly?

MARY: Of course I'm sure.

The door slams. MARY *goes back to reading her book. The door opens.* UNCLE MYERS *comes back out and stands in the doorway.*

UNCLE MYERS: Mary—

MARY: Yes, Uncle.

UNCLE MYERS: I found the butterfly.

MARY: Good.

UNCLE MYERS: Would you like to know where it was?

MARY: Where was it?

UNCLE MYERS: It was under your plate. Did you take your brother's butterfly and hide it under your plate?

MARY: No.

UNCLE MYERS: Well, someone took your brother's butterfly and hid it under your plate—

MARY: It wasn't me. Why would I do that?

UNCLE MYERS: You wanted the butterfly—

MARY: But why would I take it and put it under my own plate?

MARY *starts to run away, and* UNCLE MYERS *grabs her.*

UNCLE MYERS: Admit you took it—

MARY: I will never admit I took it. You can beat me until I'm dead, but I will never admit I took it. Never ever.

She squirms out of his grasp and runs into the house. He runs after her. The door slams behind him. We can't see them, but we can hear that he's caught her and has begun to beat her. We can hear her screaming. And now we see LIL-LIAN skipping toward the house. As she comes up the stairs, she hears MARY screaming. She stops. She puts her hand up to her ear in a sort of exaggerated listening pose. Then she marches up and bangs on the door.

LILLIAN: Hey, what's going on in there? [She knocks louder.] Open up! And stop doing whatever it is you're doing, or

I'll call the police and you'll go to jail for the rest of your life!

The beating continues, and we hear MARY *screaming in pain.* LILLIAN *kicks down the door like John Wayne and reaches in for* UNCLE MYERS. *She hauls him out by his suspenders (it's an* UNCLE MYERS *doll) and flings him down the porch stairs. She leaps down the stairs after him, takes the strop from his hand, and beats him with it.*

You're a bad, bad person, Uncle Myers—

She picks him up again and flings him offstage. MARY *appears in the doorway.*

Run, Mary, run!

MARY: Where? Where should I go? *[They look around.]*

LILLIAN: We'll hide. We'll hide in this fig tree until we figure out what we're doing.

The two of them scramble up the fig tree. A beat. The branches open, and we see them now.

MARY: I can't believe you did that.

LILLIAN: I'm amazingly strong for my age.

MARY *shakes her head in wonderment.*

I saved you.

MARY: Hey, wait a minute. It was *my* uncle, and *my* house—

LILLIAN: What are friends for?

MARY: —and *my* story. And now you're the queen of it. You're always doing that!

LILLIAN: Doing what?

MARY: You always take over—

LILLIAN: I do not.

MARY: You do, too.

LILLIAN: No I don't—

MARY: Yes you do. Look at us—we're hiding in *your* fig tree. Guess what? There are no fig trees in Minneapolis!

The branches close over them. We hear a terrible thrashing noise. MARY *falls from the tree. Splat.*

BLACKOUT.

Scene 2

"Fact & Fiction"

FACT:

I'D LIKE TO INTRODUCE MYSELF
THE NAME IS FRANKIE FACT

FICTION:

HI, I'M DICK FICTION
AND FRANKLY, THAT'S A FACT

BOTH:

AT TIMES WE TEND TO TANGLE
THERE'S FRICTION IN THE ACT

FACT:

'CAUSE "FICTION" PLAYS IT FAST AND LOOSE

FICTION:

AND "FACT" IS SO EXACT

BOTH:

BUT WHEN WE DO OUR NUMBER
IT'S SOMETHING OF AN ART
AND NOW AND THEN THEY EVEN SAY
IT'S TOUGH TO TELL US APART

FACT:

FACT

FICTION:

> AND FICTION

BOTH:

> COMIN' TO YA WITH A SONG AND DANCE
> TAKIN' FOCUS WHILE WE GOT THE CHANCE
> SEE THE DAPPER DANCIN' FELLERS
> EACH CAN BE THE BEST O' SELLERS

FACT:

> FACT

FICTION:

> AND FICTION
> WHAT'S IT LIKE TO BE IN SUCH GOOD TASTE?

FACT:

> HOW'S IT FEEL TO KNOW YOU'RE "LOOSELY BASED"?

FICTION:

> FACT'LL OFTEN ACT OFFICIOUS

FACT:

> LEAST I'LL NEVER BE FICTITIOUS

BOTH:

> WE'VE BEEN BOOKED AT THE PALACE
> WE'VE BEEN BOOKED IN DULUTH

FICTION:

> ONCE I SOLOED IN DALLAS

FACT:

> THINLY DISGUISING THE TRUTH

BOTH:
    WE'RE

FACT:
    FACT

FICTION:
    AND FICTION

BOTH:
    AND SINCE YOU'RE COMFORTABLE WITH WHICH IS WHICH
    SOME PERFORMANCES WE PULL A SWITCHEROO
    FACT MAY IN FACT BE FICTION
    OUT OF HIS JURISDICTION
    SOMETIMES, IN FACT, THERE'S FICTION, TOO

FICTION:
    WHAT IF I USE POETIC LICENSE?

FACT:
    BETTER TO USE A NAKED FACT

FICTION:
    WHAT IF IT NEEDS EMBELLISHING?

FACT:
    A FRAUD IS A FRAUD

FICTION:
    WHAT IF IT TAKES A FIB
    TO GET THE FOLKS TO APPLAUD?

FACT: *[To the audience.]*
> PLEASE, I BEG YA, DON'T PROVOKE 'IM
> ALL YOU'LL EVER GET IS HOKUM

FICTION:
> WHAT IF I CHANGE THE NAMES A LITTLE?
> WHAT IF I FEEL THE NEED FOR TACT?
> WHAT IF HER NAME IS EVA AND I CALL HER YVONNE?

FACT:
> WHY WOULD YOU CALL IT FICTION WHEN THE FICTION IS
> "NON"?

FICTION:
> FACT IS GETTIN' KIND O' CRANKY

BOTH:
> SAIL ALONG WITH DICK AND FRANKIE

BOTH:
> WE'VE BEEN BOOKED IN THE CACTUS
> WE'VE BEEN BOOKED IN THE SNOW

FACT:
> I'M A STICKLER FOR PRACTICE

FICTION:
> I MAKE IT UP AS I GO *[They dance.]*

BOTH:
> IT'S WORTH ALL THE CONSTANT FRICTION
> WORTH EV'RY CONTRADICTION
> WORTH IT WHEN FACT AND FICTION BOW

WHEN WE TAKE A BOW
LET'S HEAR IT FOR FACT AND FICTION NOW

Scene 3

Rich and famous.

LILLIAN: Rich.

MARY: Famous.

LILLIAN: Much more famous.

MARY: Much less rich.

LILLIAN: You said it, sister.

MARY: And much less famous. But famous. *[Beat.]* In 1963 I published a best-seller called *The Group*. It was made into a movie. It was a novel about a group of women who'd gone to Vassar together—

LILLIAN: —viciously reviewed by some of your closest friends. In 1969 I published my first memoir—

MARY: You were washed up as a playwright—

LILLIAN: It was a best-seller called *An Unfinished Woman*—

MARY: I went to Vietnam and wrote about the war—

LILLIAN: No one read it. I wrote another best-selling memoir called *Pentimento*.

MARY: "Pentimento" is Italian for "I couldn't really remember, so I just made it up."

LILLIAN: A chapter in it, called "Julia," was made into a movie—

MARY: We'll get to that shortly. I went to Washington to write about Watergate—

LILLIAN: Did you? I'd forgotten that if I ever knew it. I wrote another best-seller about the McCarthy period. It was called *Scoundrel Time*—

MARY: —in which you canonized yourself. I lived in Europe with my fourth husband, and I really didn't think about you much at all. I mention this because people are going to think we spent our lives thinking about each other—

LILLIAN: We didn't. Whole years passed when I didn't think of you at all. You were, after all, gone.

MARY: I was in Paris.

LILLIAN: A diplomat's wife. Passing out cheese puffs for the deputy consul of the Norwegian Embassy.

MARY: I was madly in love.

LILLIAN: Always a mistake to fall in love if it means giving up a rent-stabilized apartment in New York City. Always a mistake to choose love over your career—

MARY: I didn't give up my career—

LILLIAN: But you gave up the world you were part of. It was an awful world, worth giving up, but it was the world you'd lived in your entire writing life. While I stayed in the thick of things—

MARY: And became a celebrity.

LILLIAN: Well, don't say it as if you didn't want a piece of it. You even did a *People* magazine interview. "America's first lady of letters," in *People* magazine.

MARY: I was trying to sell a book.

LILLIAN: And you took a pop at me in *People* magazine. The interviewer asked you, "What do you have against Lillian Hellman?" Implicitly saying, "Why keep attacking her?" Why did you?

MARY: Because you were such a fraud.

LILLIAN: Nonsense. You were just using me to show off your sharp little tongue. It was lucky for you that I stayed as famous as I did, or you'd have to have found someone else to attack. You virtually sharpened your tongue on my reputation. I was your whetstone. I was part of your routine. "What do you have against Lillian Hellman?" And you answered—

MARY: "Well, I never liked what she writes."

LILLIAN: But it turned out you hadn't seen most of my plays, and you hadn't read my books, either—

MARY: I'd read as much of them as I could. I read that silly story in *Pentimento* about the turtle—

LILLIAN: What was wrong with the story about the turtle?

MARY: Who could believe a word of it? You and Hammett kill a turtle, you slice its head off, you leave it in the kitchen to be made into soup, and it somehow manages to resurrect itself and crawl away. The next day, when it turns up dead somewhere on your vast property, the two of you have a fantastically elliptical, cutthroat debate over whether the turtle is—correct me if I'm putting words into your mouth here—some sort of amphibious reincarnation of Jesus.

LILLIAN: Everyone liked that story.

MARY: Every word of dialogue in it is cocked up, but of course there's no way to prove it because everyone is dead, including the turtle. You never wrote about anyone until they were dead and were no longer around to correct you—

LILLIAN: And you never wrote about anyone unless they were alive and you could hurt their feelings. You barely even bothered to change anyone's name.

A beat.

MARY: We always end up this way—

LILLIAN: On opposite sides.

A beat.

MARY: And yet—

LILLIAN: What?

MARY: We both loved beautiful things—

LILLIAN: And we weren't ashamed of it. We both loved cooking—

MARY: Yes, I always heard you were a wonderful cook—

LILLIAN: I was. *[Beat.]* You took yourself out of the running. Big mistake.

MARY: You thought you could feed the beast forever. Even bigger mistake.

VOICES FROM WINGS: Miss Hellman, Miss Hellman, Miss Hellman—

LILLIAN: I can't talk about this right now. I'm late for my interview. Could I have some coffee?

MARY: *Un café, s'il vous plaît.*

LILLIAN *is surrounded by interviewers with cameras.* MARY *sits at a table in a Paris café on the other side of the stage and opens a book.* LILLIAN *turns from one interviewer to the next and smiles as she's bombarded with questions.*

INTERVIEWER #1: Miss Hellman, tell me about the fig tree—

INTERVIEWER #2: Miss Hellman, did Hammett help you with your writing?

INTERVIEWER #1, #2, AND #3: *[Together.]* Tell us—

INTERVIEWER #1: —about Sophronia—

INTERVIEWER #2: —about your imaginary playmate—

INTERVIEWER #3: —what "pentimento" means—

INTERVIEWER #1: This ad—advertising ranch mink—what in the world is that about?

LILLIAN: I don't know. *[Laughs.]* I don't know.

On the scrim we see a photograph of LILLIAN *as the legend in the "What Becomes a Legend Most" Blackglama mink ad, as* LILLIAN *poses and preens for the camera and the photographers shout—*

INTERVIEWER #1: This way—

INTERVIEWER #2: This way—

INTERVIEWER #3: Over here—

INTERVIEWER #1: I want to know why you did that ad.

LILLIAN: *[Laughs.]* I got talked into it one bad afternoon. Why? Do you object to it?

INTERVIEWER #1: No, but I don't quite know what to make of it.

LILLIAN: I don't blame you.

> LILLIAN *now sits for a television interview, smoking a ciga-*
> *rette. We see her image projected onto the scrim behind her*
> *as the interview progresses.*

INTERVIEWER: Miss Hellman, the story of you and your friend Julia is about to be made into a movie. Tell us about her.

LILLIAN: Julia was a childhood friend who moved to Vienna to study with Freud and became active in the anti-fascist underground. In 1936 she called and asked me to bring money—fifty thousand dollars—to Berlin.

INTERVIEWER: Money that was to be used to save people from the Nazis.

LILLIAN: Yes. She knew that I was afraid of being afraid and might be willing to do something dangerous. So I brought her the money.

INTERVIEWER: In the lining of a fur hat.

LILLIAN: Yes. I met Julia in a restaurant near the Berlin train station. I knew she'd been wounded in a demonstration, but when I saw her, and I saw the crutches, I realized she'd lost a leg. . . .

INTERVIEWER: Did you ever see her alive after that day?

LILLIAN: Never. She was murdered by the Nazis. I went to London and brought her body home to America. She'd left her daughter for safekeeping with friends in Alsace, and I never went looking for her—

INTERVIEWER: Her daughter, Lilly.

LILLIAN: Yes. I suffered terribly for not looking for the child. Hammett always said I got my worst nightmares from not looking for the child. *[She starts to cry.]* I'm sorry. I'm sorry. This has never happened to me.

All the technicians and makeup people rush in with boxes of Kleenex. LILLIAN *dries her eyes, and more makeup is applied.*

INTERVIEWER: Are you all right, Miss Hellman? Do you want to stop—

LILLIAN: No. I'll be fine.

And now we see MARY, *in the café in Paris, being interviewed by a very young* REPORTER *with a very low-tech tape recorder. This* PARIS REPORTER *puts a cassette into the recorder and presses record.*

PARIS REPORTER: Just a second. *[Into the machine.]* Testing one two three four. Sorry about this. I always do this because I'm sure it's not going to work.

The PARIS REPORTER *presses the rewind button, and the machine rewinds. The* PARIS REPORTER *presses the play button. The machine says: "Testing one two three four."*

I once interviewed Leslie Caron, and the machine didn't work, so I lost the whole thing. Which is why I bring a notebook, just in case, but then I usually forget to take notes. *[Pressing the record button.]* All right. All set. *[Picks up the recorder to make sure the tape is spinning, sets it down.]* You are not at all what I imagined—

MARY: Really. What did you imagine?

PARIS REPORTER: I don't know. I mean, I saw *Julia* recently.

MARY: Who is Julia?

PARIS REPORTER: The movie. It's based on this Lillian Hellman story. Jane Fonda, Jason Robards. And I thought you were going to be more like—

MARY: Like Jane Fonda?

PARIS REPORTER: No, no. But—

MARY: Surely not like Lillian Hellman?

PARIS REPORTER: I don't know. You're so ladylike . . . you'd hardly guess . . . you're Mary McCarthy, if you know what I mean.

MARY *lights a cigarette.*

Cigarettes. That's more like it. *[Fumbling with the notebook.]* I guess you didn't see *Julia.*

MARY: No, I didn't.

PARIS REPORTER: Oh, it's great. It's about how Lillian Hellman smuggled all this money into Germany in a fur hat and saved people from the Nazis.

MARY: Mmmmmmm.

PARIS REPORTER: Did you read *Scoundrel Time*?

MARY: No . . . although I did read about it—

PARIS REPORTER: She stood up to Senator McCarthy, you know.
   She was the only one, really. She said, "I cannot fit my conscience into your expectations." Something like that.

   MARY *exhales smoke straight at the reporter.*

   What do you think of her?

MARY: Lillian Hellman? I can't stand her. *[She smiles.]*

PARIS REPORTER: Really? Gosh. Why?

MARY: I first met her at Sarah Lawrence—*[To the audience.]*
   Blah blah blah—*[Back to the* PARIS REPORTER.*]* John Dos
   Passos—*[Back to the audience.]* Blah blah blah—*[Back to
   the* PARIS REPORTER.*]* D-O-S P-A-S-S-O-S. Two "S's"—

PARIS REPORTER: Thank you.

MARY: . . . didn't like the food in Madrid—*[Back to the audience.]* Blah blah blah—*[Back to the* PARIS REPORTER.*]* She
   was just brainwashing those girls—it was really vicious.
   And so somebody like that writes a book like *Scoundrel
   Time,* and I think that it's still scoundrel time as far as she's
   concerned. It's as if she thinks she's the only person who
   behaved morally during the McCarthy period. Everything
   she writes is false, including "and" and "but."

   MARY *smiles again. Big smile this time, the smile you smile
   when you say something funny for the very first time and it's
   a surprise to you. The* PARIS REPORTER *looks down at the
   tape recorder to make sure it's working.*

Is that working?

PARIS REPORTER: Yes.

MARY: Good.

The PARIS REPORTER *exits and we're now in New York.* MARY's *college friend* ABBY KAISER *sits down. Like* MARY, *she is dressed like a garden-club matron.*

ABBY KAISER: How's it going?

MARY: No one's said a thing. Never a good sign, I'm afraid, so it's probably not selling at all. But I'm going to be on *Dick Cavett*. He's going to do two shows.

ABBY KAISER: Two! Oh, Mary, that will help, won't it?

MARY: Let's hope so. Does anyone watch it?

ABBY KAISER: Less so now that it's on public television, but the advantage is that everyone who watches it buys books, so you're reaching the people you want to, the core audience, I think it's called. What are you going to say?

MARY: I don't know. I have to come up with something clever, I suppose.

ABBY KAISER: You always say the cleverest things—

MARY: *You* think they're clever.

ABBY KAISER: They *are* clever. They're famously clever.

MARY: I did an interview in Paris a few months ago—

ABBY KAISER: I saw it. In that little English-language newspaper.

MARY: You saw it?

ABBY KAISER: Someone sent it to me. Someone I know who knows I went to Vassar with you, who sends me everything about you. . . .

MARY: It was not a very nice article.

ABBY KAISER: I know.

MARY: The writer kept comparing me to Lillian Hellman. I had no idea that's what he was going to do. All about dashing Lillian Hellman and frumpy me.

ABBY KAISER: Can you imagine? Well, you can't let things like that bother you.

MARY: Oh, I don't, really. *[Beat.]* He wrote that I looked like a garden-club matron. *[Beat.]* But I said something funny in it, I think. About Lillian Hellman. I said, "Everything she writes is false, including 'and' and 'but.' "

ABBY KAISER: Yes, that *is* funny. *And* clever. "Everything she writes is false, including 'and' and 'but.' " That's good, Mary.

MARY: Do you think I should say it? On *Dick Cavett*?

ABBY KAISER: Sure. How do you do that?

MARY: Do what?

ABBY KAISER: Say it? Do you just sort of pop it in?

MARY: Dick Cavett has to ask me a question that it's the answer to.

ABBY KAISER: How do you get him to do that?

MARY: They call you ahead of time and ask you what you want to talk about.

ABBY KAISER: Oh, is that how they do it? I'm so stupid. So he says, "What do you think of Lillian Hellman?" Like it just crossed his mind?

MARY: Well, that's a little obvious. More like "What writers do you think are . . . overrated?" or something.

ABBY KAISER: And then you can say, "Lillian Hellman, everything she writes is false, including 'and' and 'but.'" Amazing. I had no idea.

A beat.

MARY: Do you think I should say, "Everything she writes is false, including 'and' and 'but,'" or should I say, "Everything she writes is false, including 'and' and 'the'"?

ABBY KAISER: Gosh, I don't know. They're not too different.

MARY: *[Trying them both.]* Everything she writes is false, including "and" and "but."
Everything she writes is false, including "and" and "the." *[Beat.]* I think if I say "'and' and 'but,'" people might be confused by the word "but," but if I say "'and' and 'the'"—I mean, obviously I'd have to pronounce it

"the"—*[Sounding like "thee."]*—as opposed to "the"—
[Sounding like "thuh."]—so people will be able to hear
what I'm saying—*[Beat.]* I don't want to have to make little
quote marks with my fingers.

ABBY KAISER: I always do that.

MARY: "The" is better, I think. It's so much more devoid of mean-
ing than "but," if you see what I mean.

ABBY KAISER: I "see." *[She makes little quote marks and laughs.]*

MARY: Do you think "Everything she writes is false" or "Everything she writes is a lie"—

ABBY KAISER: Including " 'and' and 'the' " or " 'and' and 'but' "?

MARY: *[Trying out other possibilities.]* "Everything she writes"?
"Every word she writes"?

A pause while MARY *thinks about this.*

ABBY KAISER: What are you wearing?

MARY: I don't know. Probably something matronly.

They both laugh.

ABBY KAISER: Are you nervous?

MARY: No, of course not. It's just a television show that almost
no one watches, right?

ABBY KAISER: Absolutely.

Scene 4

The Dick Cavett Show. *January 25, 1980*

MARY *is being interviewed by* DICK CAVETT. *Her image is pro-jected on the scrim behind her.*

On the other side of the stage, a television set hangs from the ceiling over a bed. LILLIAN *is next to the bed in a bathrobe, smoking a cigarette.*

LILLIAN: I was watching, you know. I saw you say it.

> *She climbs into the bed. We see the bed from the back, so that what we mostly see is a headboard with a curl of smoke rising above it.*

DICK CAVETT: Are there any writers you think are overrated?

MARY: The only one I can think of is a holdover like Lillian Hellman, who I think is tremendously overrated, a bad writer, a dishonest writer, but she really belongs to the past. . . .

DICK CAVETT: What is so dishonest about her?

MARY: Everything. But I said once in some interview that every word she writes is a lie, including "and" and "the."

> *And now* LILLIAN *rises up in the bed like Frumasera, and we have some fantastic visual effect of a giant black beast rising up and causing a BLACKOUT.*

Scene 5

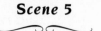

Voila.

We hear a doorbell ringing, and now we see the suggestion of a Paris apartment as MARY *walks toward the door and opens it. A* SUMMONS SERVER *stands there.*

SUMMONS SERVER: Madame Mary McCarthy?

MARY: Oui?

SUMMONS SERVER: Voila.

He hands her the summons. She looks at it.

BLACKOUT.

Scene 6

Imaginary friends.

The fig tree again.

The ENSEMBLE *sings a reprise of "Fig Tree Rag."*

ENSEMBLE:
> AND ONCE AGAIN WE SEE THE FIG TREE
> THAT BIG FIG TREE
> UP ABOVE
> AND ONCE AGAIN WE VISIT FIZZY
> WHO'S ALL DIZZY
> AND IN LOVE
> BUT NOW WE GET A VARIATION
> A MUTATION
> IF YOU WILL SHOW US THE SCENE AGAIN
> RUN THE ROUTINE AGAIN
> LOOK AT WHO'S BACK ON THE BILL
>
> FIZZY AND MAX
> THEY'RE GONNA DO THE FIG TREE RAG
> I WANNA DO THE FIG TREE RAG
> WITH YOU

The door to the house in New Orleans opens, and FIZZY *comes out. She sits on the front porch and takes out a fan and starts to fan herself with it. The branches of the fig tree part, and we see* LILLIAN *and* MARY *sitting in it.*

MARY: Very Tennessee Williams.

LILLIAN: You don't like the fan?

MARY: It just seems derivative.

LILLIAN: But it's a hot day—

MARY: Lose the fan.

MAX HELLMAN, LILLIAN's *father, comes from around the back of the house and looks at* FIZZY *as she sits there.* FIZZY *turns and sees him. She drops the fan with a huge clatter.* MAX HELLMAN *tips his hat.*

FIZZY: Max! What a surprise. When did you get back?

MAX HELLMAN: Train just got in. Beautiful morning, isn't it? Even prettier now that I see you.

MARY: You know what I have never understood? Why is no one Jewish in your plays?

MAX HELLMAN: *[Singing and davening.]* Oy oy oy oy oy—

LILLIAN: Like that?

MARY: No, not like that—

LILLIAN: We didn't really think of ourselves as Jews. We thought of ourselves as southerners—

MARY: Yes, and here comes a perfect example of it—

MAX HELLMAN: What were you thinking about?

FIZZY: Just now? Summertime, and my mama's hummingbird garden. Sarah and I used to sit still as statues on the stone bench and see if we could get the birds to buzz around our heads. Once I put a piece of honeysuckle in my mouth—

MAX HELLMAN *suddenly kisses* FIZZY, *a long, passionate kiss.*

MARY: The kiss, on the other hand, is good, if only because it gets her to stop talking.

LILLIAN: I give up. You write the scene.

MARY: All right. I will.

> MARY *and* LILLIAN *cover themselves with the branches of the fig tree.* MAX HELLMAN *and* FIZZY *stop kissing.* FIZZY *slaps* MAX HELLMAN.

MAX HELLMAN: Fizzy? Why did you do that?

FIZZY: I'm practically not speaking to you, Max Hellman.

MAX HELLMAN: Why, Fizzy? Tell me?

> FIZZY *shakes her head.*

Come on, tell me.

> *He touches her gently. She softens.*

Come on.

FIZZY: You said you'd send me a postcard from Chicago and you didn't—

MAX HELLMAN: How could I send you a postcard with that nosy child of mine poking into every crevice—

FIZZY: I know. She spies on me when I'm getting dressed, and she tells lies, too, Max, she tells lies all the time, everything she says is a lie, including—

The branches in the tree start to rustle wildly.

LILLIAN: I hate you!

MARY: I hate you!

LILLIAN: I hate you more!

MARY: I hate you more!

> *And both of them fall out of the tree. Splat.* FIZZY *screams and runs off. The* MAN *playing* MAX HELLMAN *is left onstage with the two dolls. He takes off his* MAX HELLMAN *costume and starts to sing "I Would but I Can't."*

MAN:
> I CAN'T FIX THIS
> I CAN'T HELP YOU
> ALL NIGHT LONG
> I'VE PLAYED ALL THE MEN
> AND NONE OF IT HAS MADE A BIT O' DIFFERENCE
> NONE OF IT HAS EVEN MADE A DENT
> I CAN'T FIX THIS
> I ADMIT IT
> HIT IT
>
> IF I COULD MAKE YOU HAPPY
> I WOULD, BUT I CAN'T
> IF I COULD SLAY YOUR DRAGONS
> I WOULD, BUT I CAN'T
> NO NO
> I'VE GIVEN YOU MY ALL
> WHENEVER YOU WOULD CALL

I DID WHAT HAD TO BE DONE
LORD, HOW I'VE RUN
NOT TO SAY IN ANY WAY
YOU GALS AIN'T FUN

BUT IF WE NEVER DID THIS AGAIN
I'D BE FINE
AND THOUGH YOU'VE GOT YOUR TROUBLES
WHAT'S YOURS ISN'T MINE
NO NO
SO HERE'S THE NEWS
GET BACK IN YOUR SHOES
AND TAKE THIS GHOST OF A CHANCE
WE'RE HERE UNTIL YOU FIGURE THIS OUT
JUST DANCE
LET'S DANCE
LET'S DANCE
LET'S DANCE

DON'T KEEP ME PLAYIN'
EVERY TOM DICK AND BEN
I'VE RUN THE GAMUT
FROM RAHV TO HAMMETT

I LIKE A DOLL
WHO LIKES TO FOLLOW
NOW AND THEN

SO HERE'S THE THING
GET BACK IN THE RING
AND LET ME SAY IN ADVANCE
YOU'RE HERE UNTIL YOU FIGURE THIS OUT
FIGURE WHAT THE BOUT IS ABOUT

AND UNTIL YOU FIGURE IT OUT
YOU'LL DANCE
JUST DANCE
LET'S DANCE

BLACKOUT.

Scene 7

⌒◦⌒

Hellman versus McCarthy.

We see LILLIAN *and* MARY. *Both of them are older now.*

MARY: Hellman versus McCarthy.

LILLIAN: It was huge.

MARY: She sued me for two million dollars.

LILLIAN: Two point two five million dollars.

MARY: It was on the front page of *The New York Times*.

LILLIAN: They called all my old enemies.

MARY: And mine, who were suddenly my friends.

LILLIAN: At some point Norman Mailer got involved.

NORMAN MAILER *enters.*

NORMAN MAILER: If I may—

LILLIAN: Get out of here, Norman—

MARY: *[At the same time.]* Go away.

As NORMAN MAILER *disappears.*

He wrote an article—

LILLIAN: In *The New York Times Book Review*—

MARY: I knew he would be on my side.

LILLIAN: And I knew he would be on mine.

MARY: But he attacked us both.

LILLIAN: He said you were stupid to have said what you did.

MARY: He said you should drop the lawsuit.

LILLIAN: I stopped speaking to him.

MARY: So did I.

LILLIAN: And I certainly didn't drop the lawsuit.

MARY: Although you offered to if I took it all back. Your lawyer had lunch with my lawyer—

MARY *walks over to a table with a tea service on it and sits down with her* LAWYER.

MARY'S LAWYER: I had lunch with her lawyer.

MARY: Milk or lemon?

MARY'S LAWYER: Neither. Look, Mary, you don't want to go to court with this. Just to answer the papers she filed will cost thousands and thousands of dollars. So if you're willing to say something in the form of a retraction—

MARY: Something like what? *[She passes a tray of cookies.]*

MARY'S LAWYER: Something like "I didn't mean to suggest that Lillian Hellman was a liar."

MARY: But I did.

MARY'S LAWYER: I know you did. But just say it.

MARY: But it wouldn't be true—

MARY'S LAWYER: Everyone will understand—

MARY: Every day I get another letter from someone documenting yet another lie. Do you know what Gore Vidal said about her and Dashiell Hammett? He said, "Did anyone ever see them together?"

MARY'S LAWYER: You can't win the case by proving she's a liar—

MARY: Nonetheless, I am collecting her lies. I am pinning them, like dead butterflies, on a wall of cotton.

A beat.

MARY'S LAWYER: So I should call and say you won't apologize.

MARY: Never ever. I'm not sorry I said it, I'm not. I'm sorry it didn't sell more copies of my book. I'm sorry it will bankrupt me. And I'm sorry about the sleepless nights—*[She lights a cigarette; then, re: the cigarette.]*—one of my three a day—

MARY'S LAWYER: Some people love sleepless nights. Some people thrive on litigation.

MARY: Presumably they're people with more than sixty-three thousand dollars in the bank. In case anyone asks, tell them I'm sleeping like a baby. I can't apologize. I didn't do anything wrong.

MARY'S LAWYER: But you'd just be saying it to make it go away. Everyone will understand.

MARY: I could never do that. And not that it matters, but they wouldn't understand. Not in my world.

MARY stands and walks over to a table. We see a witness stand and a table on the other side of it.

We had two arguments to make in court. One was that Lillian Hellman was a public figure. If you're a public figure, you're expected to take more criticism than if you're a housewife.

She sits down at the table. LILLIAN *enters and walks over to the other table.*

LILLIAN: A public figure, according to my lawyer, is a person who assumes roles of special influence in the affairs of society. I don't try to influence anyone but my friends—

MARY: And the second argument was that you cannot treat hyperbolic language as if it's intended to be taken literally. But, of course, I did mean for it to be taken literally.

LILLIAN: Exactly. Which is why I sued you.

MARY: Here's what I don't understand—didn't you know she was going to turn up?

LILLIAN: I have no idea what you're talking about.

MARY *and* LILLIAN *sit down at the tables on either side of the witness stand. And now we hear a gavel pounding.*

ANNOUNCER: The case of Lillian Hellman, plaintiff, against Mary McCarthy, defendant.

MARY: I call Muriel Gardiner to the witness stand.

ANNOUNCER: Do you swear to tell the truth the whole truth and nothing but the truth so help you God?

The spotlight hits MURIEL GARDINER *in the witness stand.*

MURIEL GARDINER: I do.

MARY'S LAWYER: State your name, please.

MURIEL GARDINER: Muriel Morris Gardiner. Dr. Muriel Morris Gardiner—

MARY'S LAWYER: You are a doctor of—

MURIEL GARDINER: I'm a psychoanalyst.

MARY'S LAWYER: Could you tell us a little about yourself?

MURIEL GARDINER: I was born in Chicago in 1901. I was the heiress to the Armour meatpacking fortune. I was graduated from Wellesley College and studied at Oxford. I then went to Vienna to study psychiatry at the Freud Institute. This was in 1934. My first marriage had just ended, and my daughter came with me to Austria.

MARY'S LAWYER: Can you tell us what happened to you as war approached?

MURIEL GARDINER: I was a socialist, and I became increasingly concerned as the Nazis came to power. And I was in a unique position—I had both American and British passports, and considerable wealth. So I joined the anti-fascist underground, and I was able to help a number of people escape from Austria. I fell in love with a man who was a leader of the resistance, and we were married and returned to America just before World War II.

MARY: Have you ever met Lillian Hellman?

MURIEL GARDINER: No.

MARY'S LAWYER: When did you first hear of her?

MURIEL GARDINER: Soon after I came back to America. She was a well-known playwright. And for a while we had the same lawyer.

MARY'S LAWYER: In 1941 Lillian Hellman wrote a play called *Watch on the Rhine*. Did you see it?

MURIEL GARDINER: No, I didn't.

MARY'S LAWYER: Did you know that the main characters in it were an Austrian resistance leader and his American heiress wife?

MURIEL GARDINER: Really? I didn't know that.

MARY'S LAWYER: When did you hear about Lillian Hellman again?

MURIEL GARDINER: It must have been about 1972 or 1973. A friend called me on the telephone and said had I read a book by Lillian Hellman called *Pentimento*? I said I hadn't. And she said did I know Lillian Hellman? I said we'd never met. And the friend said, "You must read this book, Muriel. She has stolen your life." It was all very dramatic. So I went out and bought a copy of the book, and I read the chapter in it that was the one she was apparently referring to—

MARY'S LAWYER: The chapter called "Julia"?

MURIEL GARDINER: Yes.

MARY'S LAWYER: Could you tell us about that chapter, in your own words?

MURIEL GARDINER: Well, it's about a woman Lillian Hellman was friends with, a woman named Julia—

MARY: Was Julia her real name?

MURIEL GARDINER: No, according to the book, Lillian Hellman changed her name. Julia was a rich young American woman who'd gone to live in Austria to study with Freud—

MARY: At the exact same time you did—

MURIEL GARDINER: Yes. She began working in the anti-fascist underground—

MARY: At the exact same time you did—

MURIEL GARDINER: Yes—

MARY: And she, too, had a daughter—

MURIEL GARDINER: Yes, she did, a daughter named Lilly—

MARY: After Lillian Hellman. Presumably the daughter's name was not changed.

MARY'S LAWYER: Please continue—

MURIEL GARDINER: At a certain point in the story, Julia asks Lillian Hellman to bring some money into Germany that's to be used to smuggle people out of the country. Which she does. In a fur hat. And she meets Julia at a restaurant, and they have some caviar, and Lillian gets back on the train and goes on to Moscow, I believe.

MARY'S LAWYER: According to the story, what happened to Julia?

MURIEL GARDINER: She was killed by the Nazis.

MARY'S LAWYER: And what happened to Julia's daughter, Lilly?

MURIEL GARDINER: Killed by the Nazis.

MARY'S LAWYER: After you read "Julia," what did you do?

MURIEL GARDINER: Well, first I thought, "Who knows? Perhaps . . ." So, on my next trip to Austria, I asked my friends if by any chance they knew of any other American woman involved in the anti-fascist underground.

MARY: And did they?

MURIEL GARDINER: No. So, when I came home, I wrote Lillian Hellman a letter.

MARY: And did it say, "You've stolen my life"?

MURIEL GARDINER: No, no, heavens no, not at all. And I didn't write her the letter right away. But it kept happening. People kept coming up to me and saying, "Have you read this story? It's your story." "You must be Julia." And so forth. So I wrote Lillian Hellman to say that I was struck by the many similarities between Julia's life and my own and couldn't help being curious because I had never met her Julia. It was very polite, I assure you.

MARY'S LAWYER: Did you receive a reply to your letter?

MURIEL GARDINER: No, I didn't.

MARY'S LAWYER: Did you ever hear from Miss Hellman?

MURIEL GARDINER: Yes. Several years later. She telephoned. Out of the blue. Well, not quite out of the blue. First her psychoanalyst called.

MARY: Her psychoanalyst?

MURIEL GARDINER: Yes. I didn't know he was her analyst. He was a doctor I knew slightly. He said he was calling on Lillian Hellman's behalf to ask me to deny that I was Julia. By then my memoirs were about to be published, and there had been some publicity—

MARY: Some articles saying that you seemed to be the basis for Julia—

MURIEL GARDINER: Yes.

MARY: And how did you respond to this doctor?

MURIEL GARDINER: I said I would have to disappoint Lillian Hellman, because I had never claimed to be Julia, so I could hardly claim not to be. A few days later the telephone rang again, and a voice said, "This is Lillian Hellman." She said she wanted to meet me, perhaps we could have lunch. I said that I was sick in bed, which was true. She said that perhaps she would come to New Jersey to see me, and she said, "I would like to bring with me a very charming young man I am sure you would enjoy meeting." Well, I assumed—perhaps incorrectly—that he was a lawyer, so I said that if she was bringing a friend, I might have a friend there, too. I'm afraid it got a little silly. A few days later she called again. By then I had pneumonia, and I told her I would have to postpone the meeting. And she said, "I wanted to explain to you why I never answered your letter."

MARY: What was her explanation?

MURIEL GARDINER: I don't know. You see, she had trouble hearing me, and I had trouble hearing her, so she said she'd call me back and hung up.

MARY: When did she call you back?

MURIEL GARDINER: I don't think she ever called me back.

MARY: I have just a few more questions, Dr. Gardiner. When you lived in Vienna, did you ever smuggle cash into the country for use in your activities?

MURIEL GARDINER: It wasn't necessary. In that period, it was very simple to do bank transfers.

MARY: And what happened to your daughter?

MURIEL GARDINER: She lives in Colorado.

MARY: Thank you. *[To* LILLIAN.*]* Your witness.

LILLIAN: My witness? She's your witness. And you're welcome to her. Look what you've done—a courtroom scene, you had the audience on the edge of their seats. You could hear a pin drop. And then your witness takes the stand—"I wrote her a letter," "I couldn't really hear her," "I'm afraid it got a little silly," and how does it end? It just dribbles away in a gigantic anticlimax.

MARY: But what about what she said? What about her story?

LILLIAN: It's an amazing story. It's remarkably similar to mine, but I told mine so much better, don't you think? Someone had to tell her story.

MARY: Are you admitting you told her story?

LILLIAN: Of course not. But what if I did? Muriel Gardiner had thirty-some-odd years to tell her story. And did she? No. She just sat out there in New Jersey letting a perfectly good story go to waste. And then my book came out, and she finally told her story. Thanks to me. She got a book contract, thanks to me. And she finally wrote her book, and guess what? It's boring. The woman can't tell her own story.

MARY: She doesn't need to tell her own story—or to be famous, or celebrated, or lionized. She is, forgive me, a good person.

LILLIAN: But she's not a writer. *[To MURIEL GARDINER.]* You are not a writer. Sorry.

MURIEL GARDINER: I suppose that's true. I'm not a writer. *[Stands.]* I'm a psychoanalyst. And our time is up for today. But may I say something to you both. *[To MARY.]* Look at you, Mary. Someone once told you a lie, a terrible lie, so you made a religion out of the truth. And it turned out to be your blind spot, because you never understood how subjective and elusive and abstract truth is—you simply thought that if you could prove someone was telling a lie, you'd won. *[To LILLIAN.]* You, on the other hand, witnessed a traumatic version of the primal scene, and then you were persuaded to lie about it. So you spent your life telling lies and expecting to be applauded for it. *[To them both.]* It all seems quite hopeless. If only there were a door to slam. Good-bye.

She walks offstage. The two women watch her go. A beat.

LILLIAN: Is she gone?

MARY: I think so.

LILLIAN: A perfect example of the limits of Freudian analysis.

MARY: I couldn't agree more.

LILLIAN: Of course, there was no trial.

MARY: None at all.

LILLIAN: I died before there could be one.

MARY: And that was the end of that. The case never went to court. But by the time you died, Muriel Gardiner's book had been published, and everyone knew you'd made the whole thing up. And not just anything. You stopped Hitler. You, Lillian Hellman, stopped Hitler and saved the Jews with your little fur hat.

LILLIAN: But you didn't win.

MARY: I destroyed you.

LILLIAN: And yet the only reason you're here is because of me.

MARY: That's not true.

LILLIAN: What if it is? What if that light on your face—[She points to the spotlight.]—is shining only because you're up here with me? Who are you, anyway? You're what's-her-name who made the mistake of picking Lillian Hellman for an enemy. You're that writer I sued because you were so mean—

MARY: That's not why you sued me. You sued me for the fun of it—

LILLIAN: I do like a good time—

MARY: You sued me to bankrupt me—

LILLIAN: How could I have known you'd saved so little money?

MARY: You sued me to give yourself something to live for—

LILLIAN: All of the above. I was old and sick and blind and looking for a reason to go on getting out of bed every day, and you were as good a reason as any. I sued you so you would be awake at three in the morning, like me. I sued you so that when you looked in the mirror and saw another line on your face, you would blame me for it. I sued you so that when you went to the doctor with the next awful thing wrong with you, you would see me smiling through the X rays. I sued you to shorten your life. Did I shorten your life?

MARY: Yes. You did.

LILLIAN: Good. I'm glad.

MARY: And I'm glad I outlived you. Although I didn't want you to die. I was very disappointed there was no trial. I wanted you to lose in court.

LILLIAN: You said that at the time, and even your friends were
    horrified.

MARY: There's no satisfaction in having an enemy die.

LILLIAN: I brought out the worst in you.

MARY: I was your undoing—

LILLIAN: You were nothing more than an irritation—

MARY: I was your nemesis—

LILLIAN: You rarely crossed my mind—

MARY: You wanted to be me—

LILLIAN: You wanted what was mine—

MARY: I had a charmed life—

LILLIAN: I had a third act—

MARY: I *ruined* your third act—

LILLIAN: I *was* your third act—

MARY: Liar!

LILLIAN: Bitch!

> *They look at each other, hatred burning. They grab each
> other. And then they kiss.*

MARY: I hate you.

LILLIAN: I wish you were dead.

MARY: I am.

LILLIAN: Even so.

A beat.

MARY: I'm leaving.

LILLIAN: So am I.

MARY: I don't have to take this.

LILLIAN: Enough is enough.

MARY: Where do you think you're going?

LILLIAN: Anywhere but here.

MARY: Anywhere? But here we are.

LILLIAN: You and I.

There's nowhere to go.

Stuck—

MARY: Together—

LILLIAN: Forever.

MARY: What did we do to deserve each other?

LILLIAN: Everything, apparently.

A long beat.

MARY: Where did Goethe write "Choose your enemies well"?

LILLIAN: He didn't. I just made it up.

A moment between them.

MARY: You never did say who Julia was. All you ever said
was—

LILLIAN: Miss Hellman will reveal who Julia was at the right
time.

MARY: Well, tell us now. We're here. We're listening. *[When LIL-
LIAN doesn't answer.]* She was you. She was the person you
might have been if you hadn't been the person you were.

LILLIAN: Who would you have been? If they hadn't lied to you.
For instance.

MARY: Hard to know. A better novelist, perhaps. *[Re: Julia.]* She
was just a story.

LILLIAN: I'm just a story. So are you. The question is, who gets
to tell it?

A beat.

Was there ever a moment we could have been friends?

MARY: Hard to imagine.

And what happened to the U-boats?

LILLIAN: To the U-boats? What do you think happened?

MARY: They collided.

LILLIAN: Absolutely. They collided.

MARY: And one of them was destroyed.

LILLIAN: Possibly.

MARY: Both of them were destroyed.

LILLIAN: Possibly.

MARY: Both of them were damaged—

LILLIAN: And both of them survived.

LILLIAN AND MARY: *[Together.]* Possibly.

MARY: But which one was it? In real life? And don't tell me there's no such thing. Don't tell me there's no such thing as the truth. I don't believe that.

LILLIAN: I know you don't.

MARY: I believe in the truth.

LILLIAN: I believe in the story.

The lights go down onstage, and LILLIAN *and* MARY *stand there.*

Behind them, on the scrim, we see two lists.

On LILLIAN'S *side: "Works by Lillian Hellman," and a list of her twelve plays and four memoirs.*

On MARY'S *side: "Works by Mary McCarthy," and a list of her twenty-six books.*

BLACKOUT.

TIMELINE

LILLIAN HELLMAN

MARY MCCARTHY

1905
Lillian Florence Hellman, the only child of Max and Julia Newhouse Hellman, is born in New Orleans on June 20. "I was the sweetest-smelling baby in New Orleans," she says years later.

1911
The Hellmans move to New York, but Lillian and her mother spend six months a year living with her two aunts in their New Orleans boardinghouse.

1912
Mary McCarthy is born in Seattle on June 21, the eldest of Roy and Therese (Tess) Preston McCarthy's four children.

1918
The McCarthy family goes to Minneapolis to visit Roy McCarthy's parents. Roy and Tess McCarthy die of influenza within a few days of their arrival. Mary and her three brothers are taken to live with their great-aunt Margaret and her new husband, Myers Shriver.

1923
Mary moves back to Seattle to live with her Preston grandparents.

1925
After two years at NYU, Hellman drops out and goes to work for publisher Horace Liveright as a reader. On New Year's Eve she marries Arthur Kober, a theatrical press agent.

1929–33
McCarthy attends Vassar College. A few days after graduating, she marries Harold Johnsrud, an actor. Years later she recalled her wedding night: "As we climbed into the big bed, I knew, too

1930–31

After moving to Hollywood, Kober becomes a screenwriter, and Hellman a reader at MGM. One night during a party at Musso and Frank's on Hollywood Boulevard, she meets Dashiell Hammett, a former detective and author of *The Dain Curse* and *The Maltese Falcon.* They spend the night together, sitting in a car in the restaurant parking lot, talking about books. "A short time later," Hellman wrote, "Arthur and I separated without ill feeling and I went back to New York."

1932–34

Hellman and Hammett live together at the Sutton Hotel, managed by Nathanael West. Hammett writes his last novel, *The Thin Man,* and suggests to Hellman that she become a playwright. He gives her a story about two Scottish teachers who sued a student for libel, and it becomes the basis of *The Children's Hour.* The play is a huge hit. Hellman is twenty-nine. She begins to write screenplays for MGM.

late, that I had done the wrong thing. To marry a man without loving him, which was what I had done, not really perceiving it, was a wicked action."

1936

McCarthy, now a book critic for *The Nation,* travels to Nevada to divorce Harold Johnsrud; on the train, she meets and beds a plumbing-company executive from Pittsburgh. Upon her return, she moves to Greenwich Village and becomes a Trotskyite. "I saw all sorts of men that winter," McCarthy later writes. "I realized one day that in twenty-four hours I had slept with three. . . ." Robert Misch, a wealthy young man who became the prototype of "The Genial Host" in one of

McCarthy's stories, often invited McCarthy to his dinner parties: "The guests at those little dinners were mostly Stalinists, which was what smart, successful people in that New York world were. And they were mostly Jewish; as was often pointed out to me, with gentle amusement. I was the only non-Jewish person in the room. It was at Misch's that I first met Lillian Hellman. . . . But I may mix her up with another Stalinist, by the name of Leane Zugsmith."

1937

Hellman travels to Paris, Moscow, and Spain during the Spanish civil war. Many years later she writes that on her way to Moscow, she secretly stopped in Berlin to deliver $50,000 to a childhood friend she calls Julia, who was involved in the anti-Nazi underground.

1937

McCarthy falls in love and moves in with Philip Rahv, a Russian immigrant and writer. Along with Dwight Macdonald and William Phillips, Rahv revives *Partisan Review,* and McCarthy becomes the drama critic of the publication. Rahv takes McCarthy and several other *PR* staff members to a lunch with the eminent critic Edmund Wilson, who is known as Bunny. "Bunny," one of his friends once asked him, "how do you get all these dames into bed?" "I talk them into it, of course," Wilson replied.

1938

McCarthy marries Edmund Wilson. The marriage is stormy from the beginning. In June, after a night of drinking and physical violence on both sides, Wilson commits McCarthy to Payne Whitney Clinic for psychiatric observation. She is discharged after three weeks. Six months later, on Christmas Day, McCarthy and Wilson's son, Reuel, is born.

1939

Hellman's play *The Little Foxes* opens on Broadway. She buys a large estate in

Westchester County and turns it into a farm.

1941

Hellman's play *Watch on the Rhine* opens on Broadway. Among other things, it's about an American woman married to a man who was active in the anti-Nazi underground.

1942

Although he is forty-six and well past draft age, Hammett enlists in the American army and is stationed in New Jersey. He spends weekends with Hellman at the farm. From Diane Johnson's *Dashiell Hammett: A Life:* "One night, as Lillian was driving into town, Hammett was plastered as usual and it all seemed too much to her. He was a disgusting drunk, pawing her and leering, and when he suggested making love, something borne of her deep exasperation, of her sense of his waste of his time, of his life, of the stupidity of all this, made her say no, she wouldn't sleep with him when he was like this. She had never said no before to any of his demands or sexual whims. Tonight, simply, no. This surprised him, sobered him, shocked him. That was it, then. He loved Lily, would always love her. But he decided he would never make love to her again, and he never did. . . ."

1943

Technical Sergeant Dashiell Hammett is sent to the Aleutian Islands, where he spends the rest of the war working on

1941

McCarthy publishes a short story, "The Man in the Brooks Brothers Shirt," in *Partisan Review.* It's about a young woman named Meg Sargent who has an affair on a train with a steel-company executive from Cleveland. The story is a sensation. Delmore Schwartz calls it "Tidings from a Whore." McCarthy is twenty-nine.

1942

McCarthy's first book, *The Company She Keeps,* a collection of stories about Meg Sargent, is published as a novel.

an army newspaper. He writes letters to his "Darling Lilishka": "A goodly batch of mail came today . . . but . . . there . . . was . . . nothing . . . from . . . a . . . slightly . . . Jewish . . . she . . . playwright who forgets that Vice President Wallace said in Los Angeles, no further back than February 4, "The common man means to get what he is entitled to." And there is no commoner man than me, and I know what I am entitled to. Think that over, sister. Meanwhile, much love."

1944
Lillian Hellman goes to Moscow on a cultural mission. She begins an affair with a young American diplomat named John Melby.

1945
McCarthy and Edmund Wilson are divorced. McCarthy testifies that Wilson abused her throughout the marriage. Wilson testifies that McCarthy attacked him constantly and tried to set fire to his office: "She would confuse me with the uncle she'd been sent to live with after her parents' death. She was under the impression— which must have been exaggerated— that her uncle had beaten her every day."

1946
McCarthy marries Bowden Broadwater and continues to write theater reviews. Reviewing Eugene O'Neill's *The Iceman Cometh,* she writes: "To audiences accustomed to the oily virtuosity of George Kaufman, George Abbott, Lillian Hellman, Odets, Saroyan, the return of a playwright who—to be frank—cannot write is a solemn and sentimental occasion."

1948

While teaching at Sarah Lawrence, McCarthy goes to hear Hellman speak. They have a fight.

1949

The Cultural and Scientific Conference for World Peace, known as the Waldorf Conference, is held in New York. A parade of Soviet artists, including Dmitry Shostakovich, appear to testify to Joseph Stalin's benevolence. Lillian Hellman sits on the dais and is identified in newspapers as pro-communist; Mary McCarthy is in the audience with her friends Elizabeth Hardwick and Robert Lowell, as anti-communists.

1951

Blacklisted in Hollywood, her income greatly reduced, Hellman sells her farm in Westchester County. Hammett serves six months in federal prison for refusing to name the financial contributors to the Civil Rights Congress.

1952

Hellman appears before the House Un-American Activities Committee and refuses to name names. In a letter to the committee read by her lawyer Joseph Rauh, she writes: "I cannot and will not cut my conscience to fit this year's fashions." She takes the Fifth Amendment when asked if she was ever a member of the Communist Party.

1949

McCarthy publishes a new novel, *The Oasis,* about a group of intellectuals in a utopian community, and Philip Rahv threatens to sue her.

1954–57

McCarthy publishes *A Charmed Life, Venice Observed,* and *The Stones of Florence.* She writes a critically acclaimed memoir, *Memories of a Catholic Girlhood,* and her uncle Harry threatens to sue her.

1960

Traveling through Europe for the State Department, McCarthy meets American diplomat James West. Both are married. "My love for Jim is increasing 'till I am quite dizzy," she writes to her closest friend, Hannah Arendt. To Bowden Broadwater she writes: "You will not believe how painfully sorry I am that I have done this to you. Can't you, can't you fall in love with someone else and remember me as I remember you?" Within a year McCarthy and West divorce their spouses and marry in Paris.

1961

McCarthy publishes *The Group,* a novel about eight Vassar graduates. It receives a mixed critical reaction and is savaged in a *New York Review of Books* parody written pseudonymously by McCarthy's friend Elizabeth Hardwick. The novel is a huge best-seller and becomes a movie directed by Sidney Lumet. Several of McCarthy's classmates threaten to sue her.

1961

Hammett dies in Hellman's Manhattan town house, where he has lived for three years.

1964

From Lillian Hellman's *Paris Review* interview: "[Mary McCarthy] has accused you, among other things, of a certain 'lubricity,' of an overfacility in answering complex questions. Being too facile, relying on contrivance." Hellman: "I don't like to defend myself against Miss McCarthy's opinions, or anybody else's. I think Miss McCarthy is often brilliant and sometimes even sound. But in fiction, she is a lady writer, a lady magazine writer. Of course, that doesn't mean she isn't right about me. But if I thought she was, I'd quit."

1969

Hellman's memoir *An Unfinished Woman* is published. It's a critical success and a best-seller.

1973–74

Hellman's memoir *Pentimento* is published. It, too, is a best-seller. The rights to one of the chapters, "Julia," are sold to MGM. Jane Fonda is cast as Hellman and Vanessa Redgrave as Hellman's childhood friend Julia. Lillian Hellman receives honorary degrees from Smith, Yale, and NYU.

1976

The third volume of Hellman's memoirs, *Scoundrel Time,* about the McCarthy period, is published and is a best-seller. Lillian poses for the "What Becomes a Legend Most?" Blackglama mink ad.

1977

Julia is released. Lillian appears onstage at the Academy Awards and receives a standing ovation.

1967–73

McCarthy and James West live in Paris. McCarthy covers the Vietnam War and the Watergate hearings as a journalist and publishes *Birds of America.*

1980

Appearing on *The Dick Cavett Show* to promote *Cannibals and Missionaries,* McCarthy calls Lillian Hellman a liar. "Everything she writes is a lie, including 'and' and 'the,'" she says. Hellman sues McCarthy, Cavett, and WNET and asks for $2.25 million in damages. Joseph Rauh warns Hellman against suing: "If this ever got to court, they could bring up every word you ever wrote or said and examine it for its truthfulness. Do you really want that?"

1983

Muriel Gardiner's book, *Code Name Mary,* is published.

1984

McCarthy asks Judge Harold Baer to issue an order of summary judgment dismissing the suit on the grounds that Lillian Hellman is a public figure. Baer refuses, instead ruling that Hellman is not a public figure and that in any case,

McCarthy's remark "seems to fall on the actionable side of the line, outside what has come to be known as the 'marketplace of ideas.'" Less than two months later, before the suit comes to trial, Hellman dies. In September, before receiving the MacDowell Colony medal, McCarthy tells *The New York Times:* "If someone had told me, 'Don't say anything about Lillian Hellman because she'll sue you,' it wouldn't have stopped me. It might have spurred me on. . . . I didn't want her to die. I wanted her to lose in court. I wanted her around for that."

1989
McCarthy dies.

ALSO BY NORA EPHRON

HEARTBURN

*"Funny and touching . . . proof that writing well
is the best revenge."* —Chicago Tribune

Is it possible to write a sidesplitting novel about the break-
up of the perfect marriage? If the writer is Nora Ephron,
the answer is a resounding yes. Seven months into her preg-
nancy, Rachel Samstat discovers that her husband, Mark,
is in love with another woman. The fact that the other
woman has "a neck as long as an arm and a nose as long as
a thumb and you should see her legs" is no consolation.
Food sometimes is, though, since Rachel writes cookbooks
for a living. And in between trying to win Mark back and
loudly wishing him dead, Ephron's irrepressible heroine
offers some of her favorite recipes. *Heartburn* is a sinfully
delicious novel, as soul-satisfying as mashed potatoes and
as airy as a perfect soufflé.

"Great fun. . . . Though Heartburn *bristles ferociously
with wit, it's not lacking in soul."*
—The New York Times Book Review

Fiction/Literature/0-679-76795-9

VINTAGE CONTEMPORARIES
Available at your local bookstore, or call toll-free to order:
1-800-793-2665 (credit cards only).